Preparing for and
Fostering Harmony
In Marriage

by Reverend
GEORGE SUKHDEO

 FriesenPress

Suite 300 - 990 Fort St
Victoria, BC, V8V 3K2
Canada

www.friesenpress.com

Copyright © 2017 by Reverend George Sukhdeo
First Edition — 2017

All rights reserved.

No part of this publication may be reproduced in any form, or by any means, electronic or mechanical, including photocopying, recording, or any information browsing, storage, or retrieval system, without permission in writing from FriesenPress.

ISBN
978-1-4602-9336-2 (Hardcover)
978-1-4602-9337-9 (Paperback)
978-1-4602-9338-6 (eBook)

1. RELIGION, CHRISTIAN LIFE, LOVE & MARRIAGE

Distributed to the trade by The Ingram Book Company

TABLE OF CONTENTS

Foreward	vii
Acknowledgements	ix
Introduction	xi

1
God's Purpose for Marriage	1
Reflecting His Image	3
Completing One Another	6
Multiplying and a Godly Legacy	7

2
Challenges to God's Purpose for Marriage	10

3
Before You Say "I Do"	18
Be Not Unequally Yoked	19
Compatibility is Important	21
Families Must Be Like-Minded	22
Prospects in Life Must Be Attuned	24
Pre-Marital Counselling Should Be a High Priority	26

4
Communication - First Level: Understanding	30
Time	31
Trust	32
Transparency	34
Listening: Seeking to Understand	35

5
Communication - Second Level: Resolving Conflict — 41
One Stone at a Time Can Build a Dividing Wall — 46
Resolving Conflict Requires Humility and Forgiveness — 49

6
Communication - Third Level: Sexual Intimacy — 53
All of Us Have Different Ideas, Expectations and Fantasies About Sex — 53
Creating Friendship — 58
Lasting Commitment — 59
Deepening Passion — 60
Exploring Sexual Intimacy — 61
Sexual Union — 62
The Beginning of a Sexual Relationship Requires Wisdom and Sensitivity — 64

7
God's Plan for Harmony — 68
God Met Adam's Needs by Creating Eve — 70
"Leaving and Cleaving" is the Responsibility of Both Parties — 72
God Uses Our Natural Differences to Build Harmony — 74

8
The Husband's Role in Facilitating Harmony in Marriage — 76
Love as Christ Did — 79
Lead Like a Servant — 80
Husband's Leadership and Responsibility in the Home — 82
Leadership in Marriage Should Be Sensitive, Caring and Gentle — 82

9
The Wife's Role in Facilitating Harmony in Marriage	85
Loving Your Husband	87
Encouraging Your Husband	89
Respecting Your Husband	92

10
Blended Families	94
Discipline	98
Time Spent Together	99

11
Money Management and Budgeting	102

12
Leaving a Godly Legacy	112

Conclusion	120

Foreward

This is an engaging book on not only finding and keeping harmony in a marriage, but equally important for those considering marriage. Unlike so many other books on this subject, which try to capture readers with drive-through pop psychology or spiritual sound bites, it offers a deeply challenging path based on Christian doctrine with no compromise. This book is for those seeking a lifetime process of knowing and serving God, as well as the spouse entrusted to them within the covenant of marriage; it is also for individuals and couples who are dedicated and searching for sound answers to the complex relationship challenges that can arise in our ever-changing world.

Tom Colwell,
Director of Credential Health Network, Western Ontario District Pentecostal Assemblies of Canada

Acknowledgements

The thought of writing this book came to me on October 7, 2012. At first I felt conflicted within and struggled with the idea, since my own marriage was not ideal. However, I was taken back to the fact that God uses us all, and the Bible is full of records of imperfect people. King Solomon—though he was the wisest person of his time—was not perfect, yet God used him to write the books of Proverbs, Ecclesiastes and Songs which have been, and still are today, a blessing to all who read them. There was also King David, who committed serious sins, but God referred to him as a man after His heart, and 50 per cent of the book of Psalms was written by him. The apostle Paul humbly declared in Philippians 3:13-14 (GW): "Brothers and sisters, I can't consider myself a winner yet. This is what I do: I don't look back, I lengthen my stride, and I run straight toward the goal to win the prize that God's heavenly call offers in Christ Jesus." In other words, he said he was not perfect, but was working toward it. Paul's writings are recorded in fourteen of the twenty books in the New Testament. Last but not least, Rahab the hooker, call her a lady of the evening, if you please, or a streetwalker. Yet the Bible has her listed among the faithful in Hebrews 11. Having conceded these facts, I realized I do not have to be perfect before I write a book of this nature. Hence, I accepted the mission.

Since no one is perfect, most marriages are not likely to be ideal, yet couples can still enjoy harmony in their marriage if they are willing to humble themselves, diligently apply the Bible's instructions and follow God's plan for their marriage.

The content of this book was drawn from the Bible, wisdom contained in Christian writings, my professional experiences as a Christian counsellor, and my personal experiences in forty-six years of marriage.

I am grateful to God for His word, the teachers who have contributed over the past years in helping me to gain knowledge and godly wisdom, my wife Shirley who in her unique way has been a motivator in times of discouragement, and finally, you who are reading this book and giving me the opportunity to share the nuggets gathered.

Introduction

Marriage comes in many worldly packages: civil ceremonies, religious ceremonies, polygamist traditions, common-law marriages, same-sex marriages, and more. Each "definition" or idea of marriage comes with its own diverse activities and rituals. In most cases, a legal marriage certificate that is signed by both parties and an officiant, and then filed with the government, gives the married couple certain governmental rights and privileges such as tax breaks and legally shared property. A marriage recognized by a corporation can give partners equal access to medical, dental and other health insurance benefits.

Obviously marriage comes with personal benefits, and drawbacks as well. It gives a person someone to lean on spiritually and emotionally, and to meet physical and financial needs, from sharing meals to shouldering large debts such as mortgages, student loans and other financial obligations. It also provides a framework for building a shared life and raising a family. Because you have a partner, marriage makes it easier to face whatever life throws your way. Of course, marriage also means compromise. It means making decisions with someone else in mind, instead of just yourself. It means not only having someone to help you with your load, but you helping your partner to meet his or her needs. It means paying the bills, keeping the home clean, and taking out the garbage. Marriage requires you to put

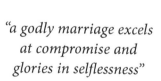

"a godly marriage excels at compromise and glories in selflessness"

someone else into your life's equations and deal with the ensuing challenges.

However, that is the world's understanding of marriage, not God's definition according to the Bible. God is the first party in the marriage. A godly Christian marriage does not thrive in an atmosphere of self-centredness. It is not a common contract like many secular marriages are, but rather a blood covenant with Jesus Christ in the centre. Sensitive to the spirit of Christ within us, we yield to the promptings of His inspired words of guidance, which always conform to the written principles of marriage contained in the Bible. A marriage with Christ at its centre is much more than having someone to do the dishes after dinner, take care of you when you're sick, help you financially or meet other needs: a godly marriage excels at compromise and glories in selflessness.

Before you get married, you must take the time to learn about God's biblical plan and principles for marriage. You must understand how it affects you, what it means for your relationship, and most importantly, how to implement His plans in your life for ultimate harmony in your marriage. Throughout this book, I will present biblical truths about marriage that are absolutely necessary for you to get everything out of marriage that God intended, as well as for you to put into the world through your marriage everything that God desires to do through you. You must not rush into your marriage. Instead, be patient, spend quality time, seek godly wisdom, have diligent deliberation with people who love and care for you, and seek the leading and confirmation of the Holy Spirit. He will help you make the right choice that will lead you into a happy, fulfilled and purposeful marriage that blesses humanity and pleases Him.

1

God's Purpose for Marriage

Everything that you've heard about marriage up until this point may be crowding your mind as you get ready for the awesomely momentous stage of life, or you may already be in a conflicting marriage and want to foster harmony in your relationship. You may be feeling inadequate from all the advice you've received about being the perfect mate. You may be feeling anxious and doubtful due to all the divorce horror stories or negative comments from those whose marriages or other relationships have failed. What may be more threatening is if your own parents' marriage was painful, miserable or ended in divorce. You may be so focused on the wedding day that you haven't really considered the normal challenges that will follow after you say "I do" and start living together. If any of these statements are true for you, take a moment to clear your mind of all your preconceived ideas and plans There is one very important truth you need to focus on above all else.

Marriage was not our idea. It did not come from the mind of mankind. No, marriage is a blood covenant, born in the heart of God, and it is a foundation established by Him. It is only in and through His grace and guidance that we can succeed at marriage. By pursuing God's design for marriage, we will experience the joy, happiness, true success and fruitful life He envisions for us. However, if we fail to pursue God's purpose and plan, marriage can be miserable and end in disaster. Thankfully God provided us with a simple guide for this incredible relationship he envisions.

What is God's design? It is for marriage to be the primary social institution for all human life on earth. It is for marriage to be the seedbed of human relationships for as long as the earth exists. It is for a life-long relationship between two people: one man and one woman. And most importantly, it is for true unity and oneness between those two people. This oneness God desires for marriages does not happen on its own. Maturing into relational unity requires both the dedication and the development of intimate personal relationships on two levels by both parties. The first necessary relationship each person needs is vertical: an intimate personal relationship with our God, our Creator. This relationship extends next into the horizontal, allowing the building of an intimate relationship with your partner.

The relationship with God is the primary foundation of the personal relationship between husband and wife. Without that foundation, we cannot hope to have the intimate, healthy relationship with our mate that both God and we intend. Instead of the flow of joy and harmony, a husband and wife will experience difficult challenges until their relationships with God are as they should be. The marriage will only be as strong as the parties' relationships are with God. When the relationship with God weakens, so does the relationship in the marriage. It grieves the heart of God to see His beloved creation, His very own people, hurt each other by not following His simple guide. God has three primary purposes for marriage. Marriage is meant to reflect His nature and character, to enable a male and female to complete one another, and to create a godly legacy by multiplying.

Reflecting His Image

In Genesis 1:26-27 (NIV), we see that God created man in His image and His likeness, which means in His nature and character, and that everything we say and do should reflect His image into the world.

> Then God said, "Let us make man in our image, in our likeness, so that they may rule over the fish in the sea and the birds in the sky, over the livestock and all the wild animals, and over all the creatures that move along the ground. So God created mankind in his own image, in the image of God he created them; male and female he created them."

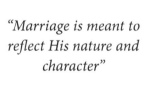

"Marriage is meant to reflect His nature and character"

This image and likeness in which we are created does not mean that man literally looks like God. Rather the image we were created in and that we are meant to reflect is a representation of God's nature and unchangeable character. In order to enter a marriage and make it successful, we must live out the nature and character of God in us as we relate to our partner. We must allow God's sacrificial love, kindness, patience and forgiveness to flow through us, instead of giving in to our carnal nature and showing selfishness, arrogance, impatience, lack of forgiveness, etc. In attempting to reproduce the likeness of God, marriage partners should never give in to their impulses to act inappropriately or be easily provoked.

Unseemly behaviour and derogatory or vulgar language should never be a way of communication. When spouses behave in an ugly way or use such manner of communication, it's obvious they are trying to demean the other person and glorify themselves instead. In doing so they are releasing destructive energy in the relationship. Whether they realize it or not, they are not only hurting and damaging their partner, but they are also doing harm to themselves and their relationship. If not dealt with appropriately, these behaviours can leave painful wounds and affect the relationship for the rest of their lives. It is vital to stick to the golden rule as stated in Matthew 7:12 (NKJV): "Therefore, whatever you want men to do to you, do also to them, for this is the Law and the Prophets."

Men and women who display God's likeness do not keep track of their partner's mistakes or wrongdoing; they do not rejoice in their failures or in unrighteous behaviour, such as their own anger or their partner's. Instead they rejoice in truth and believe that better is yet to come as God continues the good work he has started in their partner. They stay hopeful through challenges and endure "all things."

"Men and women who display God's likeness do not keep track of their partner's mistakes"

As a note, while God's forgiveness extends to all sins and ours should as well, the Bible does provide for those human circumstances that we can forgive but no longer endure. Do not mistake the call to stay hopeful and endure as a call to stay in an abusive relationship or to accept a spouse's infidelity. In these situations, you should immediately seek help from your pastor and/or a professional pastoral counsellor. Biblical counselling can, in many cases, help your marriage to heal from the wounds and pain that these behaviours can cause. If there has been any physical abuse, law enforcement should be called upon for protection and help.

God has plans for humanity and marriages: marriages are the central part of His plan—and that includes your marriage. We are to be His agents to fulfil His plans. God made both male and female humans so that we could become co-creators with Him to reproduce and raise other human beings who will also grow in Him and reflect His character and nature. This will be accomplished as we live righteously according to His manual for marriages, which is contained in the Bible. If we fail in this, we will cause pain in many ways. We will hurt ourselves and our marriage. We will hurt the heart of God, and we will hurt our children, grandchildren and possibly even many generations of our family yet to come.

Harmony within marriage is attainable. Throughout the Bible, God gives us rules and expectations not only specific to marriage, but also regarding all of our relationships with others. It is through these writings on relationships that we can understand how our marriages should be practised. Couples who follow God's plan for their marriage will experience oneness and harmony with each other. They will experience a taste of heaven on earth through the joys, happiness, fulfilment and fruitfulness of their marriage. On the other hand, when a couple runs into problems or painful experiences in marriage, it is a clear indication that the marriage is not functioning according to God's plan and the guidelines He has laid out. In such situations, one or both parties are breaching the standards set by Him either knowingly, unknowingly or through weakness or arrogance. The inevitable pain in these situations usually causes a couple to look for some solution to their troubles, and this is the time to seek out professional godly guidance and not

"Couples who follow God's plan for their marriage will experience oneness and harmony with each other"

to try to bring resolve through their own knowledge or worldly wisdom.

In the beginning of the Genesis 1:26-27 passage cited above, God gives us an example of the kind of oneness that we should strive for in our marriages. When He says "Let us," God the Father is speaking to Jesus and the Holy Spirit, exemplifying oneness of spirit, mind and purpose within the Trinity where the Son and the Spirit follow the chain of authority. When we take a serious look at ourselves and creation all around us, we can see clearly the harmonious work of our triune God.

Completing One Another

The second purpose of marriage is for us to complete one another. We see this in Genesis 2:18 (NIV), which reads: "The Lord God said, 'It is not good for the man to be alone. I will make a helper suitable for him.'" And 1 Corinthians 11:11 (NIV) shows this as well: "Nevertheless, in the Lord woman is not independent of man, nor is man independent of woman." Some of us, both male and female, boast of how we can thrive independently of a partner of the opposite sex in marriage just because we may be doing well in our finances or our profession. This may be so, but it is not in God's agenda for humanity. We were designed to be reliant on a party of the opposite sex. Neither the man nor the woman will reach his or her full potential without the other because we were designed to be a helper to one another. Besides, we all have spiritual, emotional and physical needs. A man is skilfully fashioned by God to meet the needs of a woman, and a woman is uniquely wired to meet the needs of a man. This will only happen when they first submit to God and each other. If we try to live independently of God and each other, we will be hanging loose in an open world, vulnerable to destructive circumstances and without the hope of living life to our full potential.

It is therefore essential to understand what completing one another means. Primarily it means considering our spouses first, trying to help them experience wholeness and happiness, and encouraging them to meet their purpose in life. Being self-centred and pursuing ambitions without considering your spouse's feelings, desires, happiness and well-being will destroy a marriage rather than contribute to harmony. Harmony with your mate is part of the oneness God desires for all of us, and without it we will experience loneliness, isolation, abandonment, abuse, infidelity and the ruin of our relationships. That oneness we strive for leads to the completion of one another, and achieving it requires that each spouse contribute 100 per cent of their ability to make the marriage and the home a happy place. This means both parties must be transparent, faithful and accountable to the other in every area of their lives. They must spend quality time together on a daily basis and share their challenges, hopes, dreams, faith, fears, successes and failures, all without fear of condemnation. Couples who seek to mutually complete each other will experience oneness with God and harmony in their marriage.

Multiplying and a Godly Legacy

In the book of Genesis, man is commanded to populate the earth, something that happens from within a marriage:

> God blessed them and said to them, "Be fruitful and increase in number; fill the earth and subdue it. Rule over the fish in the sea and the birds in the sky and over every living creature that moves on the ground."
> Genesis 1:28 (NIV)

Although the secular world would argue that marriage is not necessary for procreation, the fact is that independently man and woman are not properly equipped to raise children. They need the help of God, each other, a healthy extended family and the church community. A child's early understanding of unconditional love and marriage must be modelled by his or her parents in their godly home. Marriage is the opportunity and privilege of being one with God and with a partner. It is joining with Him in accomplishing His eternal plan and purpose for marriage through the ages by modelling the relationship for the next generation and the one after that. Without oneness and harmony, a marriage will be fragile and easily broken. This will cause pain to the entire family.

"harmony… will… pass… on as an inheritance to their children"

The roles of husband and wife will be best understood by children who observe their parents living out these roles in the home. They will learn to respect that God is first in the chain of authority. Next is the husband acting as priest, provider and protector, and then his wife, his "better half," functioning as his helper. Most often women do not get enough credit for the extraordinary range of tasks they may undertake to allow the family to function well. Yet children who do not see a harmonious and godly marriage modelled by their parents are being set up for a difficult life, one without understanding and appreciation of their sexual identity and eventual role in their own marriages. More destructively, the lack of harmony can erode their self-image and generally affect their life in a negative way. Couples who follow God's guidelines will experience a greater measure of oneness and harmony with their mates and within their homes, and will able to pass that on as an inheritance to their children.

Summary

Marriage is a covenant of God, not of men, and only by adhering to God's design can you achieve a happy marriage. There are three primary purposes of a godly marriage:

1. To reflect His image. Within marriage, mankind is meant to reflect God's unchangeable character.
2. To complete each other. Men and women were not intended to survive independently; by joining in marriage, both spouses can reach their full potential.
3. To multiply to create a godly legacy. In Genesis 1:28 (NIV), God commanded man to "be fruitful and increase in number." Marriage allows couples not only to populate the earth, but to raise children in a positive environment that shows them how to follow God's will.

2

Challenges to God's Purpose for Marriage

Satan has challenged God's purpose and plans for marriage from the very first union. Lucifer was the name given to Satan before the recreation of earth. He was a magnificent entity and angel of great authority, talents and gifting, second only to God. By breaking the chain of authority and rebelling against God, his name was changed to Satan, the serpent. Before creation, he was focused on God's eternal plans, which include godly marriage. After his rebellion, however, he attacked Adam and Eve's marriage in an effort to sabotage the chain of authority that God designed for marriage, and most importantly of all, God's plan for humanity.

"Satan… after his rebellion, continued with his agenda"

God in His awesome plans prepared the earth: the water, land, humans, fish, animals, vegetation, etc. He also gave human beings rules by which they and all their descendants could live a wonderful eternal life. He then placed them in the Garden. Satan, the deceiver and corrupter, whom God cast out of heaven after his rebellion, continued with his agenda and visited Eve in the garden while Adam got too engaged in domestic chores. In Genesis, we read:

> Now the serpent was more crafty than any of the wild animals the Lord God had made. He said to the woman, "Did God really say, 'You must not eat from any tree in the garden'?"
>
> The woman said to the serpent, "We may eat fruit from the trees in the garden, but God did say, 'You must not eat fruit from the tree that is in the middle of the garden, and you must not touch it, or you will die.'"
>
> "You will not surely die," the serpent said to the woman. "For God knows that when you eat of it your eyes will be opened, and you will be like God, knowing good and evil."
>
> When the woman saw that the fruit of the tree was good for food and pleasing to the eye, and also desirable for gaining wisdom, she took some and ate it. She also gave some to her husband, who was with her, and he ate it. Genesis 3:1-6 (NIV)

From the above scripture, we glean five important truths:

1. The serpent, the reincarnate Lucifer, referred to by some as Satan, was "more crafty than any of the wild animals." Genesis 3:1 (NIV) He is still a liar and deceiver, and sometimes he will even appear as an angel of light in some form or other, pretending he means to do good when he is really setting you up for a fall. This is one of the reasons we must maintain a personal, intimate relationship with God. God speaks to us by His Spirit, continually, through our hearts. He will whisper

and remind us of the right path. In Isaiah 30:21 (NIV), He declares: "Whether you turn to the right or to the left, your ears will hear a voice behind you, saying, 'This is the way; walk in it.'" And Psalm 23:3 (NKJV) reads: "…He leads me in the paths of righteousness for His name's sake." He will not only speak to us, but also empower us when we call upon Him for help.

2. The woman (Eve) lacked knowledge because Adam, the head of the household, failed to communicate adequately. He allowed himself to be too much consumed with his daily responsibilities of tending the garden or other activities of lesser importance than his marriage, and he failed to spend essential quality time with Eve, sharing the rules of the garden and being more together with her as he should. Because he didn't share with Eve the principles of life God had imparted to him before her creation, the serpent was able to lie to her about what God had said regarding the trees in the garden.

3. Before eating the fruit, Adam and Eve were already formed in God's likeness. This means that, contrary to what the serpent told Eve, their eyes were already opened. It was only after eating the fruit that they became spiritually blind and could no longer understand and view things as God does. They became emotionally damaged and mostly blinded to the ways and will of God, and their bodies were poisoned.

4. Both Adam and Eve ate the fruit, but Eve was not aware of what God had commanded regarding the fruit since she was not yet formed when He gave instructions to Adam. Adam was aware, but failed to inform Eve, and ate the fruit anyway, committing high treason that brought a curse to all humanity.

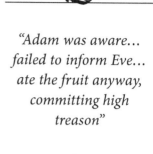

"Adam was aware... failed to inform Eve... ate the fruit anyway, committing high treason"

5. Man today, as the head of the family, bears the greatest load of responsibility in the household. As priest, provider and protector, he should seek and find the truth, leading his family in the path of righteousness according to God's will.

Adam willfully disobeyed God, choosing independence rather than submitting to authority, and from that decision, humanity has suffered at least three consequences throughout history:

1. Mankind's image of God and humanity were marred when Adam and Eve ate the fruit God told them not to; man became spiritually blind. From that moment forward, we no longer saw, understood things, and thought as God does. Instead, we see ourselves as lesser than we were created and we continue to believe the lies told to Eve by the serpent, that we were created not fully after the likeness of God as stated in Genesis 1:26. Like Adam, we distance ourselves from God, believing we are unworthy of His love and renewed relationship because of our failures.

2. Marital companionship has been threatened by two powerful forces.

    - *Blame.* Genesis 3:12 (NIV) reads: The man said, 'The woman you put here with me—she gave me some fruit from the tree, and I ate it.' Today the blame game practised by the first man Adam in that moment in the Garden continues with every ensuing generation. Man is rarely willing to accept his responsibility when he fails to be the priest, provider and protector of his family. He will point his finger in every direction but his own, never realizing that while he points elsewhere, his thumb is pointing directly back to him. If we acknowledge the thumb—acknowledge our own failure and guilt—and start searching our souls, then we will hear God speaking to us, giving us words of guidance. When we listen, hear and obey Him, things will change for the better.

    - *Competition.* Genesis 3:16 (NIV) states: "To the woman he said, 'I will make your pains in childbearing very severe; with painful labor you will give birth to children. Your desire will be for your husband, and he will rule over you." Like Adam, Eve failed also. She entered into a discussion with Satan behind Adam's back on a topic she did not have adequate knowledge of, accepted his lies, and ate the fruit before talking to Adam. Genesis 3:6 (NIV) reads: "When the woman saw that the fruit of the tree was good for food and pleasing to the eye, and also desirable for gaining wisdom, she took some and ate it. She also gave some to her husband, who was with her, and he ate it." The curse of insubordination and disobedience was released on Eve. According to Romans 13:1-2 (NLT): "Everyone must submit to governing authorities. For all authority comes from God, and those in positions of authority have been placed there by God. So anyone who rebels against authority is rebelling against what God has instituted, and they will be punished." Eve ate the fruit before consulting with Adam; she should have asked for his opinion or permission before she ate. What would the world look like today if both Adam and Eve had accepted their failure? If man had not eaten the fruit, he would always rule with godly wisdom and love. If Eve had not sinned, women would always submit in humility and meekness and be the ideal helpers God intended. Instead, the residue of Eve's rebellious nature causes a tendency toward rebellion, which results in competition for the position of authority within a marriage.

3. A godly legacy has been challenged by a godless legacy. Genesis 4:8 (NIV) tells us: "Now Cain said to his brother Abel, Let's go out to the field. While they were in the field, Cain attacked his brother Abel and killed him." Abel was the one who pleased God by bringing the best of his flock as a sacrifice, while Cain brought fruit as an offering, which showed no respect to his Creator. Satan tried to destroy Abel's legacy by convincing Cain to murder Abel. Cain in his unrighteousness killed his godly brother, something that humanity still echoes today as the godless try to silence the godly and end their legacy in this world. This practice takes place in marriages today due to the lack of knowledge of God's will and the deception of Satan.

Satan's plan is threatened by couples who are becoming one with God and each other in their plans of marriage. Unity of mind and purpose for God's will strengthen a marriage to leave a lasting legacy of godliness in the world, as well as mirroring stronger, wholesome qualities to our hurting world. Therefore Satan concentrates major attacks on married couples. Ephesians 6:12 (NIV) reveals: "For our struggle is not against flesh and blood, but against the rulers, against the authorities, against the powers of this dark world and against the spiritual forces of evil in the heavenly realms." There exist in this world both visible and invisible realms, and this verse tells us that the forces of the invisible realm are always active. This means we must be vigilant, never ignorant, and resist the strategies of the forces of unrighteousness. At the same time, we must maintain balance and live a righteous life as God wills, especially in marriage.

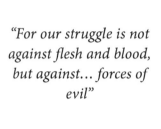

"For our struggle is not against flesh and blood, but against… forces of evil"

Each individual's marriage is much more important than he or she may think. It affects God's reputation and eternal plans because it is the foundation on which His vision is built. We must recognize that our marriages are taking place on a spiritual battlefield, rather than on a romantic balcony, as the world would have us picture. God's purposes reveal that our mates are our co-workers and friends, not enemies or competitors. This is the way we must try to see our mates and accept them as God's gift to us. His purposes can be accomplished only when we follow His manual, the Bible, for our entire lives. When we fail to do that, we become victims of our enemy. If we succeed, though, and we follow God's manual, we become victors for Him. Proverbs 13:15 (KJV) states: "Good understanding giveth favour: but the way of transgressors is hard."

Summary

1. Satan has challenged God's purpose for marriage since he deceived Adam and Eve in the Garden of Eden.
2. Eve was not the only one to blame for the temptation of the serpent. As head of the household, it was Adam's responsibility to share God's principles of life with Eve. His failure made it possible for Satan to deceive her.
3. Three of the consequences suffered by mankind since Adam's disobedience are:
   - Man became spiritually blind; instead of seeing ourselves as created in God's own image and likeness, we now see ourselves as less than what God created us to be.
   - The forces of blame and competition were allowed to threaten marriage.
   - The godly legacy Adam and Eve were created to uphold has been threatened by Satan's godless legacy. This has continued from Cain's murder of Abel through to the present day.

3
Before You Say "I Do"

With a clearer understanding of God's plans and purposes for marriage, it is imperative that you carefully examine the kind of relationship you are planning or expecting to have. Spend the quality time required to establish a clear vision of the most important part of your life, decide how to prepare yourself for the life-long commitment, and make the right choices.

"Spend the quality time required to establish a clear vision of the most important part of your life"

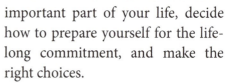

At this stage, you may already have a spouse in mind or you may be in a serious relationship and engaged to be married. Regardless of what stage you are at, there are at least four important factors that you should consider before committing to a marriage. Prayerfully use the following considerations as a tool to sift out the incompatible more quickly. This will save you much time in searching.

As Christians, we believe the most important decision in our life is accepting Jesus Christ as our Lord. When we do, the Spirit of God enters and resides in our hearts. The second most important decision we will make is the choice of our lifetime partner. We take risks on a daily basis by the choices we make, whether we are conscious of them or not. We do so when crossing the road, riding the subway, driving our automobile, or even breathing, drinking or eating. So it is with choosing a mate. In different times and stages of life, people change for the better or worse. This makes our choice of a mate even riskier. Nevertheless, as we similarly take steps to reduce the risks of crossing the street by careful observation of the traffic lights and flow of traffic, we can reduce the risks involved in selecting a life partner by using biblical principles, godly wisdom and His spirit within us as guidance.

Having Christ in your life, and being sensitive to the voice and promptings of His spirit from within, will help you make better decisions. As you maintain communion with Him, you will find He is always guiding and giving you discernment to make the right choices in every area of your life, including choosing your spouse. His written word in the Bible will always confirm what His spirit is saying and must always be used as final authority. The problem of wrong choices remains today: we are often led by our worldly ambitions, carnal passions, or by something or someone else.

Be Not Unequally Yoked

In both the Old and New Testaments, God's chosen people were cautioned to choose mates of the same faith. Deuteronomy 7:3 (NASB) reads as follows: "Furthermore, you shall not intermarry with them; you shall not give your daughters to their sons, nor shall you take their daughters for your sons." This is added to by 2 Corinthians 6:14 (MSG): "Don't become partners with those who reject God. How can you make a decision between right and wrong? That's not partnership; that's war."

That charge remains for believers today. It's not simply an ideal we should strive for, but rather a direct command given for a good reason. One should not even date an unbeliever. In doing so, you will increase the risk of a miserable marriage and possibly a divorce, sooner or later, if there are no changes in the unbeliever's heart. A relationship with an unbeliever, with someone of different faith or belief, may seem good in the beginning. However, as compromise sneaks in, it will eventually cause strain on you, on your relationship with your Heavenly Father, and on that person because of the difference in your values and belief. Compromising God's word always leads to corruption. In Amos 3:3 (NKJV), the question is asked: "Can two walk together, unless they are agreed?"

The old saying "love is blind" is true. One can easily fall in love and, in blindness, venture into serious trouble that may last a lifetime. Additionally, the risk of getting emotionally and physically entangled once the body's chemistry takes over is very real. Few people have the ability to control themselves once they have started to fall in love, and they end up compromising their beliefs or desires in order to stay with a person they should not be with. For many, it is difficult to accept that compromise is a possibility in major life decisions such as raising children in a specific faith or even staying steadfast in one's beliefs. However, when the time comes to compromise on big issues, it creeps up on the back of smaller issues, like skipping devotions or church attendance to go to a ball game or wrestling match or more seriously going to an exotic vacation to solve your relationship problem rather than a marriage seminar. With an "equally yoked" relationship, time together can be spent in Bible study, praying, serving in the church, or at a Christian concert. This leads to harmony and a situation where "iron sharpens iron," as stated in Proverbs 27:17 (NIV), rather than being dulled by an inferior metal.

Compatibility is Important

Compatibility is much more than simply enjoying one another's company or having things in common. Important factors to consider include temperament, moral values, spiritual maturity, religious denomination, level of education, cultural background and racial views, among others. For instance, if one party has a very laid-back, easygoing temperament and the other needs strict order and schedules to feel comfortable, they could be positive influences on each other. However, just as easily, they could end up unintentionally hurting each other and the relationship simply by living lonely, separated lives. Two Christians from different denominations may think they will sail easily through life based on their shared love of Christ, but if one comes from a denomination that places high importance on pacifism and the other comes from a long line of military men, it could easily cause serious tension in the relationship. Spiritual maturity is particularly important, as one could consider oneself to be equally yoked to another Christian, when in reality the spiritual maturity levels are so far apart that the relationship may be aggravated by misunderstandings, feelings of inferiority/superiority, or even just impatience with the other person's spiritual walk.

For the sake of long-term compatibility, it is important not to fall into the trap of idealism. Instead, face reality right from the start. Remember outward beauty is only skin-deep and the true quality of a person is on the inside of his or her heart and mind. Much time must be spent in communication in order to truly know the person who lives in that body. Adequate communication enables people to see each other's invisible dimensions. Once each party gets a clear enough view

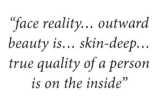

"face reality... outward beauty is... skin-deep... true quality of a person is on the inside"

of the real person on the inside, they come closer to making a better decision.

After all of that is established, it is still important to make sure a couple shares a majority of personal likes and dislikes. While these are not the foundation blocks of a relationship, having these things in common eliminates the risk of living separate lives by pursuing separate hobbies, passions and entertainments. Sharing even the smallest parts of a life together helps to create the oneness in a successful and harmonious marriage. Childhood experiences, relationships with parents, teenage challenges, relationships with the other sex, past successes and disappointments, serious health conditions and hopes for the future should all be discussed so that there are no skeletons jumping out of the closet at any later point.

Families Must Be Like-Minded

Family compatibility is another important factor to consider when choosing a spouse. Both parties must examine their religious beliefs to determine exactly what they are and what their levels of spirituality are. Do both families have the same beliefs about divorce? Do they consider it an option? And if so, under what conditions? What is their position on abortion? What about racial discrimination and identity issues?

Family history is important, as well. Has there been a trend of divorce, infidelity or abortion in either family? Has there been an addiction to alcohol or substance abuse of any kind? These weaknesses can run from one generation to the next, if not intercepted. Children of divorced parents can have a host of issues, ranging from not being able to trust a spouse to lacking an understanding of spousal communication, roles and more. If children grow up watching an unhealthy marriage, what will their understanding of marriage be when they are old enough to marry? What are the expectations of each party based on what was learned in childhood? Children of divorce can have low expectations of marital success or they can suffer from unreasonably high expectations that grow out of a desire to avoid reliving the pain they have witnessed and of which they have been a part.

What is each family's mother/father relationship like? Was it harmonious or contentious, competitive and combatant? Were alcohol and/or drugs part of the family's challenges? If so, how did it affect the family? Even a couple that stays married can have a negative relationship that impacts their adult children in harmful ways. If a man's father was abusive—verbally or otherwise—to his mother, he may be stuck in a destructive pattern he doesn't even recognize. If the woman is also verbally or physically abusive it will damage also. If a woman's mother was never willing to submit to her father, that woman may not know what submission looks like. If a parental relationship is intact but strained, the children of that union will have a difficult time fostering good health and harmony in their own marriages.

Family communication is also important. Do family members speak to each other politely? Are they always kind and gentle? Then that will likely be the kind of communication brought to the adult children's marriages. On the other hand, if family members are coarse, loud, argumentative, cruel or rude, that communication style is just as likely to be displayed in the relationship. Remember that the communication a person learns at home is often what he or she will resort to subconsciously, especially in times of stress.

Finally, if there is or has been any kind of abuse in the family, it is important to discuss it before entering into marriage. Any type of abuse between family members has grave effects on the entire family. Verbal, emotional, physical or sexual abuse between the parents, or between parents and children, or even between the children themselves all leave deep scars that can cause serious problems for a marriage before it even starts. These issues must be dealt with before marriage can be entered into or the marriage cannot be healthy and therefore cannot be harmonious.

Prospects in Life Must Be Attuned

To achieve harmony in marriage, it is important that a couple discuss the many options they will face together and how they will approach them. Having an established course of action will offer stability and godly unity. Discussing these options before the marriage occurs gives each party a chance to understand where the other is coming from, as well as to decide where they are and are not willing to compromise.

To that end, family planning is vital. Do both possible spouses want children? How early after marriage will they start to have children? How many children does each person want to have? Are the numbers the same or close enough so that a family can be started and so that each person will be comfortable in the future? Or are the numbers so far apart that one person will be unhappy no matter how many children the couple has? If one party finds that they can't have children, will adoption be an optional path or would they prefer to live without children? If the husband has a low sperm count will intracytoplasmic sperm injection be considered? Or if the wife is infertile will the implantation of an egg be an option? If adoption is an alternative, will it be a male or female child? Of what culture, colour or nationality will that child be?

"family planning is vital"

Career and calling are also important. If one person in a relationship is called to ministry, it is important that the other person be made aware of the calling and the sacrifices it will likely demand. Will one or both parties pursue a professional career, start their own business or work an hourly job? Will both husband and wife work outside the home or will one stay home to run the household and raise the children? Maybe both husband and wife will work, but one will work full-time and one will work part-time, or one will work outside of the home and one inside. There are many possible avenues and each must be discussed to discern the possible pitfalls, as well as the advantages. In the end, both parties must be comfortable with the plan in order to avoid resentment down the road.

Of course, there are still other questions to be considered. Where does each person want to live and how far are they both willing to move for things like careers and ministry, or to be close to family? Would each be willing to move to another city or region for the other's job? Would they consider a house in the city to shorten the commute or a home in the suburbs to be closer to aging parents? If an international move becomes an option, would both parties feel the same way about the possibility? These discussions may seem premature, but they can come up with very little warning as life progresses.

When challenges do arise, such as an inability to agree on a move or children or a job, how will each person deal with them? Do they go to the Lord in prayer, spend more time in His word and seek, find and follow His guidance? Do they consider compromise and listening to be important or overrated? If one person is more willing to listen to parents or other relatives than to their mate, that marriage is headed for trouble and discord. There are many ways people deal with conflict and it is important to know ahead of time how both you and your future spouse will approach challenges to bring resolve to your inevitable conflicts. Armed with that knowledge, you can come up with a plan suitable to both parties for those times when challenges will arise, rather than being blindsided and incapable of coming together to find a solution.

With all of these factors to consider, a couple is still not ready to head for the altar until they complete the next important step: finding someone to help them work through everything they need to address before the marriage.

Pre-Marital Counselling Should Be a High Priority

Many important factors affect a marriage, making it challenging to maintain a good relationship. In this age, married couples face an uncertain job market, the challenges of career training and often-changing careers, in addition to the competition involved in simply remaining employed. They also deal with staying healthy, raising children and keeping up with the rapid changes in a society dominated by the post-modern, high-tech generation. Statistics gathered by the American Psychological Association show that 40 to 50 per cent of marriages in the United States end in divorce, and those rates get even higher for second and third marriages. In fact, Mark Banschick's 2012 article in *Psychology Today*, "The High Failure Rate of Second and Third Marriages," puts the divorce rate for second marriages at 67 per cent and the rate for third marriages at 72 per cent. According to Statistics Canada, about 38 per cent of all marriages that took place in 2004 will end in divorce by 2035. With failure rates as high as these, it becomes even more important for couples to seriously prepare themselves for marriage or re-marriage.

Many people will spend tens of thousands of dollars and decades of their lives equipping themselves for a career, but very rarely would those same people invest that much time or finances in preparing themselves for a marriage intended to last a lifetime. Failing to engage in the proper preparation and take part in adequate pre-marital counselling may lead to a painful divorce sooner or later. After all, can you imagine jumping into the deep end of the pool or into the ocean without learning how to swim?

Would you plunge in, just hoping to figure it out once you're in deep and under the water? The choice to take the dive unprepared will undoubtedly determine whether one sinks or swims. Even though marriage is more serious than swimming, couples often enter marriage while enjoying the passionate honeymoon phase. They feel that it will last forever and never consider the effort it will take to keep the flame burning. Soon enough, though, the honeymoon phase ends and reality sets in—whether the couple is prepared or not. This is the time when they have to take off their ballroom attire, put on work boots and gloves, and use the necessary tools to keep the garden of marriage fruitful and flourishing. Some realize they are not equipped for the challenge before them. They end up being confronted with the same challenges the world today faces as they listen to the wrong people, who are sometimes their own parents, siblings, "friends" or esteemed members of society and eventually they believe divorce is the only solution.

> *"pre-marital counseling… will pay dividends far above monetary values"*

To combat the problem of giving up when the marriage gets difficult, couples should prepare for marriage by investing and completely committing to comprehensive Bible-based pre-marital counselling. If they take the step of seriously going through proper pre-marital counselling, they give themselves a better chance of making their dream marriage a reality. According to the website healthresearchfunding.org, studies show that pre-marital counselling can reduce the possibility of divorce by about 30 per cent. It is one of the most valuable investments a couple can make. It will pay dividends far above and beyond monetary values. Most will pay tens of thousands of dollars for engagement and wedding rings, tuxedos, weddings dresses and extravagant receptions. However, only a small handful will invest in the few essential hours of pre-marital or re-marriage counselling that could help them divorce-proof their marriage. No wonder divorce rates are on the increase.

Good Christian pre-marital counselling and choosing the right mate are extremely important before any marriage begins. These will help you to prepare and keep Christ in the centre of your marriage. With Christ in the centre, a marriage will be solid. Ecclesiastes 4:12 (NLT) declares: "A person standing alone can be attacked and defeated, but two can stand back-to-back and conquer. Three are even better, for a triple-braided cord is not easily broken." Also, in Matthew, Jesus shared this parable:

> "Therefore everyone who hears these words of Mine and acts on them, may be compared to a wise man who built his house on the rock. And the rain fell, and the floods came, and the winds blew and slammed against that house; and yet it did not fall, for it had been founded on the rock. Everyone who hears these words of Mine and does not act on them, will be like a foolish man who built his house on the sand. The rain fell, and the floods came, and the winds blew and slammed against that house; and it fell—and great was its fall." Matthew 7:24-27 (NASB)

Counselling before marriage, as well as before re-marriage, is an essential part of the preparation required to build a marriage on a firm foundation. Wise couples—those who wish to enjoy a happy, fruitful married life—go into marriage with their eyes wide open, truly preparing themselves for the challenges that marriages encounter. With counselling and godly wisdom, they learn more about themselves and their partner's strengths and weaknesses and how to become compatible. Some also discover past baggage that needs to be dealt with before tying the knot. They will better understand the vow of "until death do us part," be prepared to overcome the challenges that will surely arise, and reduce the risk of divorce. Though the challenges they face may be similar to those faced by other married couples, statistics reveal that couples who participate in pre-marital counselling are better equipped to deal with them. In the end, they enjoy a better marriage and family life than unprepared peers.

Summary

God's word, both written in the Bible and through His Spirit within you, will aid you in selecting the right partner.
1. Compatibility is key, and it is about more than getting along. Consider your perspective spouse's temperament, personality and cultural background before deciding to wed.
    - Choosing a mate from the same religious denomination will ensure no undue strain is placed on your relationship with God.
    - Also, consider how compatible your potential mate's family is with your ideals and life. Children of divorced or dysfunctional families may have a harder time trusting and communicating with their own husband or wife.
2. Thoroughly discuss your plans for the future with your mate before marriage. How many children do you each want? Will you both pursue careers, or will one of you stay home with the family? Is moving an option? Considering all of the eventualities before marrying may prevent unhappiness in the years to come.

Couples who take advantage of pre-marital counselling are better prepared for the challenges of marriage and tend to be happier and more successful in the long term.

4

Communication - First Level: Understanding

In Proverbs 24:3 (MSG), we are told: "It takes wisdom to build a house, and understanding to set it on a firm foundation." Effective communication involves more than talking and listening. It requires that couples seek to understand each other. Understanding each other will involve some extra effort, but a successful marriage will be built more readily if each partner is committed to diligently working on becoming sensitive and patient with the other. In the same way that your body is sustained by healthy blood pumping through your arteries, a marriage thrives when there is healthy communication. Couples who seek to understand each other need to know the essentials of engaging in healthy communication; these essentials include time, trust, transparency and listening.

"your body is sustained by healthy blood pumping... a marriage thrives when there is healthy communication"

Time

As we are reminded in Ecclesiastes 3:1 (NIV): "There is a time for everything, and a season for every activity under the heavens." Understanding someone comes from spending quality time with that person, preferably on a daily basis or as frequently as possible, with the object of getting to know them more intimately. Our understanding and intimacy can be limited by the time and effort we are willing to dedicate to them. As we all know, time is a precious commodity in our capitalistic, narcissistic and fast-paced society.

Not only are there things to do, but places to go and appointments of high priority to be kept. There are also frivolous pursuits that make claims on our limited time each day. Time is life, and when we manage our time well, we end up doing well in managing our life as a whole. After first spending time with God on a daily basis, we must spend time on our mates (and children if any), our employment, our domestic chores and then church- and community-related activities. This order of priorities is usually not very easy to keep because unfruitful thoughts and activities come up like bandits in the middle of the important tasks to rob us of our precious time. These bandits can be seriously destructive, as we are warned in Ephesians 5:15-17 (NASB): "Therefore be careful how you walk, not as unwise men but as wise, making the most of your time, because the days are evil. So then do not be foolish, but understand what the will of the Lord is."

Of all that occupies us during a day, we should be placing a high priority on time spent listening to our mates, sharing thoughts, encouraging each other spiritually, comforting each other emotionally, meeting physical needs, discussing financial and family matters, and praying with and for each other. If we do not use the available hours of the day wisely, thoughts of envy, competition, jealousy, greed, infidelity and other foolishness will arise, as well as temptations to practise ungodly behaviours such as deceit, gossip, drunkenness, substance abuse and unwise use of the internet. Harmful thoughts and practices can begin as suggestions from the evil one, and when given time to dwell on our minds, they can start to destroy our personal lives and marriages.

Trust

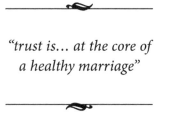

"trust is… at the core of a healthy marriage"

In order to bring intimacy into communication, trust is the next important element at the core of a healthy marriage. Your mate must have absolute confidence that he or she can rely on you, under any condition, for the rest of your lives. For that assurance to come and stay within the marriage, confidence must be earned and maintained. Private information about your mate's past, present and future that was confided to you, or any marital and financial challenges you face together, must not be discussed with others without your partner's consent, regardless of circumstances. This includes his or her weaknesses, fears and failures or the struggles being experienced in your relationship, as well as his or her faith and dreams of the future. You must not share this kind of information with your mother, father, sister, brother or best friend out of frustration or for any other reason without your mate's approval. The only exception would be in a case where supplying such information is warranted by the judicial laws of the country.

The truth is that, while we trust God and He should always be first in our lives, everyone also needs a human being to trust. That is the way we were created. And the first person any married individual should trust is his or her spouse. Therefore both mates must make every effort to establish that trust. It is important not only to have a mate who can be trusted with your whole heart, but also to be the one your mate can equally trust. If you do not make yourself vulnerable, your mate will not be comfortable making himself or herself vulnerable to you. With the absence of trust in a relationship, a void exists that will make it extremely fragile. As a human being, there will be an instinctive need to fill that gap. Like with any other void, if not filled, eventually the unfulfilled mate may seek and probably find someone or something else to fill that gap.

This ties back into everyone needing someone to trust. We are all created by God for relationships and have a built-in natural desire to share our lives with others. We all need to be open and vulnerable with someone and to feel that the person to whom we open ourselves will guard our hearts. Lack of trust can be very dangerous to a marriage. In some cases, the person your mate chooses to trust will be a friend or sibling of the same gender. If that happens, there is still a fracture in the marriage, as discussed earlier. But the problem can become even worse if the person your mate chooses to trust is someone else of the opposite sex who is not a relative.

In many cases, that "someone else" of the opposite sex may be suffering from similar issues in their marriage. If so, your already fragile relationship could be open to destruction, which can come very quickly. In other cases, though the "someone else" could have the best of intentions, he or she can still become an active participant in the destruction of your marriage. This is because whomever your spouse trusts with his or her innermost self will be the person with whom he or she will feel the closest and most comfortable. It is all too easy to slowly descend into an inappropriate relationship with someone you grow close to, even if you think you are being cautious and respectful of your spouse.

Transparency

Titus 1:15 (NKJV) tells us: "To the pure all things are pure, but to those who are defiled and unbelieving nothing is pure; but even their mind and conscience are defiled." This verse speaks of the purity of our souls, through which we perceive goodness or evil. Deception leads to corruption, but trust and intimacy are built through transparency. Transparency involves being open, honest and sincere with your spouse and others with whom you relate. Being transparent will help you to be pure from the inside out, and it will also enhance your self-image and worth. It will release you to live a life of greater freedom, comfort, confidence and creativity, without fear of what others may think because you will not have the burden of trying to deceptively hide the dark corners of your life. Living a shady life built on deception and elusiveness will first of all cause spiritual distortion, followed by the searing of your conscience and possibly even a mental breakdown or physical sickness. The anxiety that comes from a shady life will negatively affect all areas of your life and definitely communication with your spouse, thus contributing to an unhealthy dynamic.

"Being transparent will help you to be pure from the inside out, and it will also enhance your self-image and worth"

Spouses must learn to be transparent, first of all in prayer—that is communicating with God—and this will eventually assist them in becoming transparent with their mates. We must learn to share without fear and to prayerfully trust God with the consequences of our transparent living. Couples absolutely must be able to share their thoughts on fear and faith. They must be able to share opinions, dreams, aspirations and even feelings of weakness without shame, fear or condemnation. The book of beginnings speaks of nakedness: "And they are both of them naked, the man and his wife, and they are not ashamed of themselves." Genesis 2:25 (YLT) Though this scripture talks about outward nakedness, it can also be used to apply to inward honesty and openness. This kind of openness is true transparency, which rids a relationship of shame or fear by ensuring that both mates truly know and accept each other, flaws and all.

Listening: Seeking to Understand

We were admonished in the New Testament: "Remember this, my dear brothers and sisters: Everyone should be quick to listen, slow to speak, and should not get angry easily. An angry person doesn't do what God approves of." James 1:19-20 (GW) As human beings, we all need someone who cares enough to listen, truly hear and understand us. That relationship is vital. However, just as with trust, we need someone other than God, someone here on this earth, who shares our earthly life, to listen to us as well. We all need a person who will try to understand us as we honestly share about ourselves, without being fearful of judgment or condemnation.

Poor listeners exhibit certain traits that stifle communication. They have developed habits that create a cloud of misunderstanding. Poor listeners interrupt, interjecting with thoughts that aren't always relevant. They do not follow, as they should, what is being communicated and often stray in another direction. They become engaged with thoughts of something out of context or the words and actions of someone else or another scenario altogether. On the other hand, when we listen to another person with undivided attention, we get to understand and know what is really going on inside them. We get to understand the invisible dimensions of their lives. Having insight into this knowledge enables us to nurture a closer relationship.

We must listen attentively and with genuine interest to everything that is said to us if we hope to understand. If we do not clearly understand what is being said, we need to ask for clarification. We should listen without bias and with an attitude of humility and openness to discover and understand. We should not be critical or judgmental in attitude or facial expression. A good listener will have an attitude that encourages communication, understanding the following points:

1. All of us have different ways of communicating in addition to the actual spoken words we use. We will sometimes respond through silence, facial expressions or physical movements.
2. Learning about the ways your mate communicates will be essential for effective interaction and a healthy relationship. Your deeper awareness of your spouse's communication methods can reduce the frequency of disconnects in your relationship.
3. To properly understand what your spouse is communicating, you must try to listen with interest, respect, acceptance and a willingness to understand.
4. Listening should happen with the attitude that your mate is your friend and not your enemy. Because both you and your mate will need each other's help to mature and develop, a combative attitude will hinder rather than help this process.
5. If both of the partners in a marriage listen with an attitude of willingness and openness to receive what God may be trying to communicate to them through their spouse, over time they will grow closer to God and each other.
6. Good listening is helped when both partners maintain an attitude of fairness and compassion.

7. A desire for clarification and details can lead to a deeper sharing and building of trust between spouses.

Good listening increases understanding and builds unity. As we listen to each other, it is helpful to ask the type of follow-up questions that will allow your mate to more fully express his or her ideas or concerns. Questions should not be used for the purpose of refuting, but rephrasing an idea or concern that your spouse is sharing as a question can have the benefit of better clarifying a subject area or plan of action for both of you. For example, questions such as "What did you mean when you said …?" or "What do you need for me to do at this point?" can lead to clarity and good decision-making. A good listener will practise positive habits that increase communication. It is important to pay attention to what your spouse is trying to say and not the way it is being verbalized. Make an honest effort to understand, and always steer clear of criticism, insults and condemnation. It is just as important to seek to be understood by your mate as it is to seek to understand your mate. Your mate can try to understand you, but will need your help to do so. There are some main points to consider as you seek to be understood by your spouse.

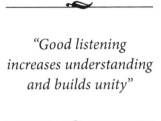

"Good listening increases understanding and builds unity"

1. As people enter marriage, they bring to the relationship unique ways of expressing themselves that may reflect cultural background and many other factors.
2. It will require patience to learn each other's methods of communication, and a lack of patience may produce stress in the relationship.
3. It is prudent to be aware of how the experiences of our childhood and later life have influenced the way each

of us responds to our spouse. In turn, it is important to respond with grace and gentleness when we see our spouse sometimes resorting to childish behaviour.

4. Poor self-image can cause fear of rejection and fear of intimacy. Each spouse should try to discover the other's level of self-image in order to be able to help overcome these fears.
5. To get closer, couples must be willing to risk opening their hearts to each other. They must express their deeper thoughts and feelings with each other, even though this may be uncomfortable at first.

Any capacity for intimacy in this life will begin with entrusting yourself to God because He made you and understands you best. Jesus invited all of us to come to him when He said: "Come to me, all of you who are weary and carry heavy burdens, and I will give you rest." Matthew 11:28 (NLT) When we learn to trust by first learning to confide in and trust God, that trust and transparency will flow into our relationship with our spouses. As you try to express your feelings and ideas to your spouse, remember that it is helpful first to clearly settle on what you want to say, and to make it as compact and respectful as you can. Also, give some thought to the best way you can present your idea. For example, should it be expressed with excitement or disappointment? Finally, decide when and where you will say what you need to say. Maybe the conversation should take place after a meal or after your prayer time — or perhaps you may want to keep it for a future visit to a park or a drive in the country. If you have children, determine if you want to have the conversation in their presence or out of their hearing.

Developing an understanding of each other in your marriage will require both good listening skills and the ability to express yourself well. Remember, God's grace, wisdom and power are available through His Spirit in you to assist you in taking the risk of being vulnerable with your mate. You should frequently assure one another that you will always do your best in trying to listen and understand. It is important that both parties express themselves freely and fully, with no interruption. Ideally, effective communication should start before marriage, not just after you say "I do" and it must continue as a life-long practice. This is one of the basic ways to experience harmony in a marriage.

Summary

1. The essentials of healthy communication are time, trust, transparency and listening.
   - Setting aside time daily to be with your spouse keeps communication open and prevents feelings of envy, competition or jealousy.
   - You and your spouse should be able to trust each other completely. A lack of trust opens a void in the relationship that can be a gateway to infidelity.
   - Transparency means being open, honest and sincere with your spouse.
   - Listen to your spouse with the goal of understanding and giving them your undivided attention without criticism or judgment.
2. It is important that both spouses in a marriage seek to understand and be understood by each other. Have the patience to learn your mate's communication style, accepting the ways they express themselves that could be different from your own.
3. If you are open and honest with yourself and with God, you will be better able to trust and be trusted by your spouse.

4. Think before you speak. Determine what you want to say, how to say it, and when it will be appropriate to say it before starting the conversation.

5

Communication - Second Level: Resolving Conflict

If you are in a relationship, you will experience conflicts. It is bound to happen. Conflict occurs when parties cannot agree on an issue and it can quickly lead to quarrelling, which can be painfully destructive and eventually build a wall between you and your spouse. Rather than avoiding conflict, however, it is something that should be confronted and resolved respectfully, decently and in a biblical manner. In Matthew 18:15 (NIV), Jesus instructed us how to take the first step in dealing with conflicts. He said, "If your brother or

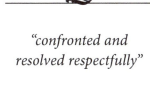

"confronted and resolved respectfully"

sister sins, go and point out their fault, just between the two of you."

Resolving your marital conflicts will require understanding a few main points. First, you must understand that conflict is common to all marriages. Therefore the goal of your marriage should not be to remain conflict-free. Instead, you should aim to handle the inevitable conflicts in beneficial ways, and most importantly in a manner pleasing to God. Resolving your conflicts will help you to mature into the nature and character of our Heavenly Father, which will in turn benefit both you personally and your marriage. With the settlement of each new conflict, your relationship will get stronger, richer and move to the next level of compatibility.Secondly, you should recognize that all marriages experience various degrees of frustration, pain and anger inflicted by the offence of one partner on the other. While the frustration, pain and anger are regrettable, marriage is one of God's ways to mature us in order that we may fulfil His destiny for our lives. We should embrace the opportunity that conflicts present us with to grow and mature. As you move forward in dealing with conflict, remember my own personal proverb: "Blessed are the flexible, for they shall inherit peace in marriage." Thirdly, remember that the choices we make during a conflict have the ability to draw us together rather than drive us apart. How? Conflicts arise in a marriage when a couple cannot agree on the challenges before them and in challenging situations it will be important to find out what will please the heart of God. Lengthy, peaceful dialogue, in which we discuss the advantages and disadvantages of the choices before us, is what will bring you to resolution. In the process, you will draw closer to one another, and greater sensitivity and respect will be developed.

When we are inevitably hurt by our mate, our tendency is to respond in one of two ways: either clam up or blow up. People who clam up will either withdraw from their mate, reject their mate, or become silent and cold; people who blow up can become aggressive, loud, hostile or even violent. Instead, we must use the Bible as our map and the spirit of God within us as our guide when we seek solutions to the conflicts in marriage. We must take time out and, when the storms of anger have drifted away, deal with the conflict without quarrelling, nagging, clamming up or blowing up.

Jesus told us what to do when someone offends us: "If your brother or sister sins, go and point out their fault, just between the two of you. If they listen to you, you have won them over." Matthew 18:15 (NIV) In the two verses that follow, He suggested that if the offender is too arrogant to accept his or her fault and ask for forgiveness, others should be brought in. If this also fails to bring reconciliation, other disciplinary actions should be taken. Facing the issue head on is just the beginning of dealing with the conflict. The process must continue with forgiveness, patience and the realization that we are not perfect either. Sometimes one or both of you will have to change or compromise.

James 1:19 (NIV) declares: "My dear brothers and sisters, take note of this: Everyone should be quick to listen, slow to speak and slow to become angry." Resolving conflict through biblical principles requires that we first understand the anatomy of anger. Anger is a God-given emotion, a surge of energy emerging from within. It is possible to use it productively, though, and that is what we must do. Don't focus on your spouse. Instead, focus on the source of the problem so that your anger can work for you rather than against you. When anger arises, withdraw mentally or physically if necessary, and spend time getting your thoughts in order about the issue. Only then should you return with grace and a positive, peaceful approach that can be a fair contribution to resolving the problem.

Anger is part of God's nature as well. What is different, however, is that God's anger is never selfishly motivated and instead is only aroused because of His love for us. God is angered when we break His rules and hurt ourselves and our families.

When we break God's rules, we break ourselves and eventually our marriages as well, so His divine anger is warranted. Divine anger can be good and healthy for us, and it can also help us to keep our mates on the right path. However, it is also an emotion that can pull people apart if not dealt with in God's way. For many people, anger is the most common response when conflict occurs. When anger is aroused, it is imperative to acknowledge and deal with it constructively. Whenever you feel anger, or you are dealing with your partner's emotions, it is important to understand not only where the feelings come from and why, but also how you can use it in a positive manner rather than allowing it to take a hurtful and harmful course.

Anger can emerge when we feel our rights have been violated or our expectations not met, or when we feel we have been hurt. Whenever our anger arises, we should not deny our anger or our hurt feelings. However, we must guard against making degrading remarks about our spouse or launch any verbal attacks against him or her, particularly not in the presence of our children, parents or friends. Instead, concentrate on seeing the issue from your spouse's point of view. Respectfully, and with the permission of your spouse, take some time out by going into another room or outside for a walk. Some people feel safer when they show anger rather than acknowledge hurt feelings, but they should be given the opportunity to express their true feelings if they can do it in a civilized way that does not hurt another person. We should all seek to understand before we seek to be understood. Because anger is also a God-given emotion that can be a motivator to resolve conflict, it is all right to feel it as long as we do not hold onto it and allow it to fester into resentment. In Ephesians 4:26 (NIV), Paul writes: "In your anger do not sin:

"a God-given emotion that can be a motivator to resolve conflict"

Do not let the sun go down while you are still angry." Therefore, when you are angry, you must let your partner know why. You should also make every effort to end your anger by addressing it promptly, and definitely before you go to sleep that night.

In Genesis, God explains how anger can become destructive: "Then the Lord said to Cain, 'Why are you angry? Why is your face downcast? If you do what is right, will you not be accepted? But if you do not do what is right, sin is crouching at your door; it desires to have you, but you must rule over it." Genesis 4:6-7 (NIV) Therefore we are told that our anger must be controlled. We have God's instruction that we must rule over it. He gave us this ability from the very beginning, yet many of us do not even attempt to bring it under control. Uncontrolled anger can result in bitterness, which can weaken our immune systems and cause our health to fail. It can cause stress in our families and affect their physical, emotional and spiritual health as well. It can raise blood pressure, cause depression and lead to conflicts of many different types. It also affects our relationship with God. It is better to tell God what we think, feel and want rather than to take our anger out on those we profess to love. Uncontrolled anger can intensify future conflicts and build up walls of isolation in ourselves, our spouses and our children. To help you control your anger, stop and take the following steps:

- Ask yourself what is making you angry and if your anger is justified.
- Ask why your anger is so intense and determine whether you are reacting inappropriately in any way.
- Be prepared to control your emotional surge by guarding your tongue and your actions, listening carefully, trying to understand those around you and taking time out if necessary; return later when you are able to engage in respectful dialogue.

One Stone at a Time Can Build a Dividing Wall

Ephesians 4:15 (NIV) consists of more than one truth for Christians in a relationship: "Instead, speaking the truth in love, we will grow to become in every respect the mature body of him who is the head, that is, Christ." Not only does Paul urge us in this verse to not shy away from conflict, but he also shows us the correct way to bring up our issues with one another. The apostle puts it very well in 1 Peter 3:8-9 (NIV): "Finally, all of you, be like-minded, be sympathetic, love one another, be compassionate and humble. Do not repay evil with evil or insult with insult. On the contrary, repay evil with blessing, because to this you were called so that you may inherit a blessing." We must humbly give in to the God-like nature in us and let Him arise and help us overcome bad behaviour with good.

"We must humbly give in to the God-like nature in us and let Him arise and help us overcome bad behaviour"

1. Use the right tone of voice when you speak. You must speak gently and with humility from your heart, without taking joy in correcting your partner's wrongs and without any hint of superiority. Be careful not to insult or embarrass your partner, particularly in front of others. Be careful what you discuss with parents, siblings and friends. Having difficult conversations in front of your partner's friends or family will likely make him or her feel as though you are ganging up and trying to shame him or her. This, in turn, makes it more likely that your partner will shut down, go into isolation or dig in, and makes it less likely that he or she will truly re-examine his or her role in the argument.

Be careful not to gossip or slander your partner. Remember your partner is God's gift to you. God has joined you together and you have become one. It is not right to express disapproval of God's gift to you; rather, give thanks. Proverbs 12:4 (KJV) refers to a woman, but I think it can apply to a man as well: "A virtuous woman is a crown to her husband: but she that maketh ashamed is as rottenness in his bones." James 3:6 (NIV) speaks to the dangers of a wilful tongue: "The tongue also is a fire…. It corrupts the whole body, sets the whole course of one's life on fire, and is itself set on fire by hell." The Message version of this passage is even more direct: "It only takes a spark, remember, to set off a forest fire." A careless or wrongly placed word out of your mouth can do that. By our speech we can ruin our lives, turn harmony to chaos, throw mud on a reputation, send the whole world up in smoke and go up in smoke with it, smoke right from the pit of hell. It is clear, from James's writing, that speaking without first thinking it through and considering what needs to be said, how it should be said, and when it should be said can and will lead us to destruction.
2. **Offer guidance with humility.** As Paul writes in his Epistle to the Galatians: "Dear brothers and sisters, if another believer is overcome by some sin, you who are godly should gently and humbly help that person back onto the right path. And be careful not to fall into the same temptation yourself." Galatians 6:1 (NLT) Use the points below to make sure you are approaching your spouse with grace, and are not tempted:
    - Determine what your motives are. You should not be wanting to control your partner or trying to get back at them. Think before you speak, and in

humility rephrase or correct what you may have blurted out in anger or frustration.
- Decide where and when the conversation should most appropriately occur. You do not want an already delicate situation to suffer additional undue strain.
- Check your heart to make sure you are as willing to receive correction as you want your spouse to be. You should be prepared for the possibility of a confrontational response, and you should be willing to listen carefully and calmly to deal with any negative responses. Remember that when you push through a swinging door it will swing back at you. Do not respond in a surprised, irrational or angry manner if or when this happens. Remaining calm will not only keep the conversation civil, but will also help you strengthen your relationship.

"agree ahead of time on the ways both of you will discuss and resolve conflicts"

Discuss and agree ahead of time on the ways both of you will discuss and resolve conflicts. Try to address only one problem at a time so that it can be resolved before you move onto another problem. For example, if you are in conflict over the grocery budget and over your partner's choice of words, first discuss one issue and then the other. Don't let the issues bleed together. Also, stay focused on the actual problem rather than on who your spouse is as a person. If your spouse is someone who does not like to help in keeping the household clean, you should discuss why cleanliness is important, and not criticize your spouse's personality or habits. Avoid calling your spouse lazy or dirty, but do ask for help with specific tasks. It is also counterproductive to blame a spouse's upbringing, family or personal attributes for the behaviours that upset you. That course of action will only serve to separate you and your partner, not bring you together. It will not help you as you try to resolve a conflict. In fact, it is more likely to cement the behaviours you are hoping to change. Here are a few more helpful ways you can frame your concerns as you begin your conversations.

1. Talk about how your spouse's behaviour makes you feel and avoid talking about what the behaviour makes you think of him or her as a person.
2. Start your sentences with "I" rather than "you." This will keep you from sounding as though you are making accusations and will encourage productive conversation.Remember that your end goal is to improve and strengthen your relationship. You should never be trying to win an argument.
3. Stick to the facts and your own observations instead of trying to judge your spouse's inner motivations. You cannot know for sure what is going on inside of another person, even if you think you know that person very well.

Resolving Conflict Requires Humility and Forgiveness

In Ephesians, Paul simplifies the challenge presented to us by conflicts, whether they are conflicts with a spouse or someone else:

> Do not let any unwholesome talk come out of your mouths, but only what is helpful for building others up according to their needs, that it may benefit those who listen. And do not grieve the Holy Spirit of God, with whom you were sealed for the day of redemption. Get rid of all bitterness, rage and anger, brawling and slander, along with every form of malice. Ephesians 4:29-31 (NIV)

The Bible teaches that we must take responsibility for how we speak with others. We must always be careful not to tear them down or diminish them in any way through the words we choose. Instead we are to build them up, thinking of who they are in Christ and how we can benefit them at the point where they happen to be in their lives. Not doing so grieves the Lord, who loves us and did so much for us. Therefore, when we are the person who has offended someone else, we must admit that we were wrong and seek forgiveness. We must be willing to say, "I was wrong. I am sorry. I should not have done that. Please forgive me?" We must be willing to repent and change our path, and speak statements such as: "I realize I hurt you. I will never do that again." We should also make a point of specifically addressing what the behaviour was that we need forgiveness for, so that the other person can have the assurance of knowing that we truly know and understand what we did.

In the Epistle of Paul to the Colossians, he counsels: "Bear with each other and forgive one another if any of you has a grievance against someone. Forgive as the Lord forgave you." Colossians 3:13 (NIV) When we are the person who is asked to grant forgiveness to another, remember that we can ask God to help us. We can speak with Him privately first because He has forgiven us for our sins.

"It will take humility and courage"

We can also know that forgiving will release us from the negative emotion of resentment or the need to get even with the other person. It will take humility and courage, but forgiveness is a choice we make to set the other person free and to allow our relationship to heal and rebuild. The following are some points we can consider as we offer forgiveness to a spouse:

- Forgiving does not mean we are pretending that the behaviour did not happen; the person asking for forgiveness

must still be accountable for future actions and must make a serious effort to regain trust.
- We must be direct, but generous and gracious as we agree to forgive and provide our spouse with such sincere statements as: "I forgive you. I am not perfect either. I would like us to settle this and start rebuilding our relationship."
- Even as we forgive and offer our spouse an opportunity to change, we should remember to remain cautious. Forgiving is only the beginning of the healing process.

How the process of reconciliation is approached is also important. If you are the offended person, approach the issue lovingly and avoid the natural tendency to rehearse the hurt. Instead, define the agreement and solution and discuss what you can do in the future to avoid a recurrence of the offence. Seeking and granting forgiveness restores harmony. If you find you and your spouse continue to disagree, pray and seek professional counsel.

Summary

1. Conflict is common to all marriages. Don't make it your goal to be a conflict-free couple, but rather seek to resolve conflicts in a way that will be both beneficial to you and pleasing to God.
2. Use biblical principles to resolve conflicts in your marriage.
3. Anger can be productive if it is aimed at the source of the problem, not at your spouse. Don't try to deny your anger. Use it to redress wrongs against you rather than to hurt your mate.
4. Approach confrontation calmly, speaking gently, and without insulting or embarrassing your partner.

5. To resolve conflict, the offending partner should seek forgiveness, while the offended should show compassion in granting it.

6

Communication - Third Level: Sexual Intimacy

All of Us Have Different Ideas, Expectations and Fantasies About Sex

Sex is God's idea. Sex facilitates communion and oneness. It is an interaction through which deepest correlation is established. The rhythms of back and forth are not only sensual, but open a channel through which flow the emotional, intellectual and spiritual links that knit the couple together. It is a primary bonding factor in a marriage and should be placed as a high priority. Therefore it is beneficial to acquire a good theoretical knowledge on the subject before you say "I do." This should continue after you say "I do" and during the course of your marriage, so you can enjoy each other, fulfil the purposes of marriage, and keep the spring of pleasure flowing richly in your sex life. The technique in bed is not all that matters, but the love that you have for each other and what the copulation means to each of you will make a huge difference. Using wisdom, being sensitive to your mate's needs, and using creativity in the joining together can enrich the relationship throughout your lives. Nevertheless, some may find the need of a manual for reference. The following part of this chapter will enlighten you with some important principles.

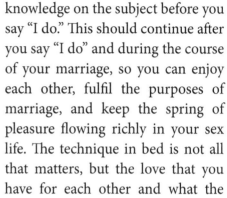

"The technique in bed is not all that matters, but the love that you have for each other"

In the first chapter of the book of beginnings, we see that our sexuality is connected to replenishing the earth with human beings: "So God created mankind ... male and female ... God blessed them and said to them, "Be fruitful and increase in number; fill the earth ..." Genesis 1:27-28 (NIV) Genesis 2:24 (GW) adds to this: "That is why a man will leave his father and mother and will be united with his wife, and they will become one flesh."

The act of sex within a marriage is a gift from God. It holds the dual purpose of establishing His kingdom on earth and providing pleasure for husband and wife. It is supposed to be one of the factors that keep two parties bonded for life. In order to maintain everything in a marriage as it should be, mates must work at enriching, maturing and preserving a healthy sex life. The primary object of each party in the coming together for sex should be to pleasure their spouse and not be selfish. Knowledge of your mate's physical needs, what turns him or her on and off, and his or her responses, along with patience, is vital. Besides, one needs to keep healthy, be kind, look attractive, be clean and smell delicious. A good sex life, like every other part of marriage, requires effort to attain and maintain, but it is effort you will never regret because it brings dividends that the greatest financial investments cannot. A healthy sexual life simply starts by being willing and available. Both husband and wife should not only have the liberty to explore and enjoy each other, but also build up, compliment and express appreciation for each other.

Healthy sex can start with such ordinary activities as shovelling snow, gardening together or simply doing dishes as subtle teasing moves the couple toward the bedroom. This can begin with body and eye language and complimentary, romantic words. In Song of Solomon 4:1 (MSG), we see romance in motion when the Solomon the lover expresses the beauty he beholds: "You're so beautiful, my darling … and your dove eyes are veiled by your hair as it flows and shimmers… Your smile is generous and full—expressive and strong and clean." Take note that Solomon starts by expressing his admiration, praising his wife for her beauty, and then sharing his deep affection. He looks at her eyes, which are the windows to her soul. He likens them with those of doves, symbolizing peacefulness, calm and innocence.

He continues to affirm and charm his wife in simple, delightful language, mentioning her other magnetic feminine qualities in Song of Songs 7:1-9 (NIV):

> How beautiful your sandaled feet,
>   O prince's daughter!
> Your graceful legs are like jewels,
>   the work of an artist's hands.
> Your navel is a rounded goblet
>   that never lacks blended wine.
> Your waist is a mound of wheat

    encircled by lilies.
Your breasts are like two fawns,
    like twin fawns of a gazelle.
Your neck is like an ivory tower.
Your eyes are the pools of Heshbon
    by the gate of Bath Rabbim.
Your nose is like the tower of Lebanon
    looking toward Damascus.
Your head crowns you like Mount Carmel.
    Your hair is like royal tapestry;
    the king is held captive by its tresses.
How beautiful you are and how pleasing,
    my love, with your delights!
Your stature is like that of the palm,
    and your breasts like clusters of fruit.
I said, "I will climb the palm tree;
    I will take hold of its fruit."
May your breasts be like clusters of grapes on the vine,
    the fragrance of your breath like apples,
    and your mouth like the best wine.

He passionately carries on, complimenting her attributes as he ventures from head to toe. A similar approach should be practised by husbands. Primarily, It is the husband's responsibility to start the flame, usually if the time is appropriate the loving wife will respond spontaneously. I believe we can learn a lot from King Solomon and his lover, who lived in the 900s BC, about how to entice our spouses. An approach like Solomon's would entice and no doubt his mate would respond eagerly. What was the

"Men were wired to lead... women... to be spontaneous"

woman's response? In Song of Songs 7:10-11 (NIV), we see her natural reciprocation: "I belong to my lover, and his desire is for me. Come, my beloved, let us go to the countryside, let us spend the night in the villages. Men were wired to lead, women were wired to be spontaneous, but when sin entered the earth, both got corrupted. In the previous paragraphs, we saw how the husband pursued his wife in a God-like manner and in return we saw the wife's spontaneous submission to his sensitive and admirable approach. Prior to her final yielding, let us look at her response in Song of Solomon 5:10-15 (NLT) as the rendezvous was initiated:

> My lover is dark and dazzling,
> better than ten thousand others!
> His head is finest gold,
> his wavy hair is black as a raven.
> His eyes sparkle like doves
> beside springs of water;
> they are set like jewels
> washed in milk.
> His cheeks are like gardens of spices
> giving off fragrance.
> His lips are like lilies,
> perfumed with myrrh.
> His arms are like rounded bars of gold,
> set with beryl.
> His body is like bright ivory,
> glowing with lapis lazuli.
> His legs are like marble pillars
> set in sockets of finest gold.
> His posture is stately,
> like the noble cedars of Lebanon.

We see that her responses were similar and attuned to his advancement. She responded naturally to his advances in words that eventually ended in the rendezvous. Like many things in life, a healthy sexual relationship starts simply with being available and willing. The husband and the wife should have the freedom to enjoy each other's bodies. The Bible is clear, not just about the pleasure awaiting married couples, but specifically about the pleasure a man can derive from just looking at his beloved. Being available is merely the starting point and is definitely not the only contribution to a healthy sex life. In order to have a rich and fulfilling sex life, a couple must have a kind and compatible relationship. A good relationship will be developed as genuine friendship grows.

Creating Friendship

"This foundation must be set before the nest is laid"

In Song of Songs 5:16 (NIV), we see friendship already established: "His mouth is sweetness itself; he is altogether lovely. This is my beloved, this is my friend…" "Sweetness," along with "lovely" and "friend" are key words she uses to describe him. Her heart probably melted, appreciative admiration was expressed, and transparency and vulnerability were established. "His words were comforting and uplifting. A true friend will stand beside and for you in every circumstance. This foundation must be set before the nest is laid. In this verse, the wife defines her husband not only as her beloved, but also as her friend. When a husband and wife are true friends, they have a relationship that can endure and overcome all the challenges that come their way. This foundation of being true friends before lovers will pave the way for a more intimate sexual connection from the deep dimensions of your souls.

Lasting Commitment

Commitment is the next layer of the foundation on which gratified sex can be experienced. Commitment originates from the inner dimensions of the human will. It should not be based on emotion, intellect or the outward look of a person. Jesus said in Matthew 19:6 (TLV): "So they are no longer two, but one flesh. Therefore what God has joined together, let no man separate." When you make vows of commitment, they are made before God and probably family and friends. God is committed to us. He is not double-minded. He is the same yesterday, today and forever. He states: "I hate those who are double-minded…" Psalm 119:113 (NASB). In addition, we learn in James 1:7-8 (NIV) that a double-minded person is unstable in all their ways. We must live up to our God-like image, have integrity, and meet our commitments. There are always ways to overcome the difficulties that married couples experience. Though there may seem to be no way, when we seek Him, He will show us the way.

In Song of Songs 8:6 (NIV), we see an example of an invitation to commitment: "Place me like a seal over your heart, like a seal on your arm; for love is as strong as death, its jealousy unyielding as the grave. It burns like blazing fire, like a mighty flame." To be placed like a seal is to be made permanent, not temporary, moveable or subject to change. In our current culture that celebrates the temporary, only permanence and commitment can truly set your marriage on the right course. Sex is a gift from God, but it is a gift meant to be experienced inside a committed, enduring relationship. By valuing the life-long commitment you have made to each other, you allow your sexual relationship to flourish in a way that only an enduring marriage can sustain. Commitment opens the door to vulnerability and passion.

Deepening Passion

Passion is resident in the heart of every human soul. It can be aroused by spiritual or emotional means and expresses itself physically. It is a force that can cause human beings to excel in their potential in every area of their life, and this is much more so with sex. Though it may ebb and flow, it will keep you on the mountaintops. We see passion deepened in Song of Songs 4:11-16 (NIV):

"Passion is resident in… every human soul. It can be aroused… and expresses itself physically"

Your lips drop sweetness as the honeycomb, my bride;
milk and honey are under your tongue.
The fragrance of your garments is like the fragrance of Lebanon.
You are a garden locked up, my sister, my bride;
you are a spring enclosed, a sealed fountain.
Your plants are an orchard of pomegranates
with choice fruits,
with henna and nard,
nard and saffron,
calamus and cinnamon,
with every kind of incense tree,
with myrrh and aloes
and all the finest spices.
You are a garden fountain,
a well of flowing water
streaming down from Lebanon.
She
Awake, north wind,
and come, south wind!

Blow on my garden,
that its fragrance may spread everywhere.
Let my beloved come into his garden
and taste its choice fruits.

This is very enticing communication, with no inhibition or hesitancy, just complete surrender, with an invitation to come in and enjoy. This will drive the average human to jump over the walls and enter the garden. Sustained and deepening passion will keep your marriage bed exciting and your sexual relationship strong.Friendship, commitment and passion combine to create an environment where a sexual relationship will flourish.

Exploring Sexual Intimacy

God has given you to each other! The world would have you believe that you cannot be sure of your marriage until you know if you are sexually compatible, but the world has the equation backwards. It is not sexual compatibility that determines the future of your love for each other. Instead, your genuine, unconditional love for each other in every area of life will help you to adjust physically in whatever ways are needed for your sexual compatibility. Remember that your physical relationship directly

"so it will grow as your love for God and each other deepens"

correlates to your emotional and spiritual relationship, so it will grow as your love for God and each other deepens. You should always give thanks to God and your mate before and after you enjoy the pleasure of this blessing. With this practice, your sexual relationship will grow, deepen and reach the highest point of ecstasy. Therefore you must tend to your relationship with care, and sexual satisfaction will follow.

It is also important that you never let outside parties, such as in-laws or friends, or any outside concerns disrupt your relationship. The Bible commands that married couples be available for each other sexually unless very specific circumstances prevent it, and those circumstances are spiritual. Yet in Ephesians 4:32 (NIV) the apostle Paul exhorts: "Be kind and compassionate to one another…" When you love and really care for each other, you are willing to compromise and be patient and consider the emotional state of your mate before you ask for sex. In 1 Corinthians 7:3-5 (NIV), the apostle Paul gives clear simple instructions: "The husband should fulfill his marital duty to his wife, and likewise the wife to her husband. The wife does not have authority over her own body but yields it to her husband. In the same way, the husband does not have authority over his own body but yields it to his wife. Do not deprive each other except perhaps by mutual consent and for a time, so that you may devote yourselves to prayer. Then come together again so that Satan will not tempt you because of your lack of self-control." Sexual impulses should, like other desires, be submitted both to your will and to God's purposes. Otherwise, they will control and frustrate you.

Sexual Union

Men and women are different in many relational ways and there are important differences to note when it comes to sexual relationships. The differences can be broken down into three categories: orientation, stimulation and needs. Orientation includes differences in what is most important within the sexual relationship for each gender. Stimulation and needs are more self-explanatory and show the contrasts in what is necessary both for the sexual relationship to take place and to make it satisfactory for both partners. The table below was cited in the workbook of the Family Life Marriage Conference:

DIFFERENCES BETWEEN MEN AND WOMEN

	MEN	WOMEN
ATTITUDE	Physical	Relational
	Compartmentalized	Holistic
STIMULATION	Body–centered	Person–centered
	Sight	Touch
	Fragrance	Attitudes
	Actions	Words
NEEDS	Respect	Security
	To be physically needed	To be emotionally needed
	Physical Expression	Intimacy
	Physical Release	Time
SEXUAL RESPONSES	Acyclical	Cyclical
	Quick excitement	Slower excitement
	Difficult to distract	Easily distracted
ORGASM	Shorter, more intense	Longer, more in-depth
	More physically-oriented	More emotionally-oriented

The Beginning of a Sexual Relationship Requires Wisdom and Sensitivity

It is important to have the right mindset about sex and to think about it from a godly perspective. Your expectations for sex may have been negatively affected or even perverted by movies, books, magazines and other secular media. Because sex is a gift from God, these outside influences are a poison to your mind and marriage.

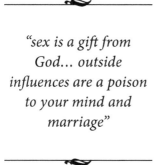

"sex is a gift from God... outside influences are a poison to your mind and marriage"

However, negative influences are not the only things that can impact your sexual relationship with your spouse. Past sexual relationships can also negatively impact the sexual relationship in your marriage. In the beginning, your spouse's feelings must be carefully considered. Wisdom and discernment are required to understand the best way to deal with either mate's sexual past. In this world, especially today's society, many people commit sexual sins freely, without any sense of guilt, before they are married. They feel that it is something they should do, and if they do, it adds value to them. The Bible teaches us that fornication—sexual intercourse between people before marriage—is a sin. However, we have a covenant with God that covers a multitude of sins and it started a long time ago in the Abrahamic covenant. Let us look back at where it started.

A study of blood covenants in the Bible will disclose that there are many of them. The major covenant, which supports all of the others, was the one between God and Abraham. Let us look at how God initiated and established the covenant. Genesis 15:9 (NKJV) states: "So He said to him, 'Bring Me a three-year-old heifer, a three-year-old female goat, a three-year-old ram, a turtledove, and a young pigeon.'" Why the three-year- old animals?

I believe their age is symbolic of the triune God: God the Father, God the Son and God the Holy Spirit. The animals were split and lined in a row as directed by God and here is what happened afterwards as written in Genesis: "And it came to pass, that, when the sun went down, and it was dark, behold a smoking furnace, and a burning lamp that passed between those pieces. In the same day the Lord made a covenant with Abram …" Genesis 15:17-18 (KJV) Take note here that after the shedding of blood, a covenant was declared between God and Abraham. The Abrahamic covenant was officially established: passing through the animals were the three parties of the Godhead and Abraham. We can see in Malachi that every true marriage is entered into by a covenant.Malachi 2:14 (MSG): "Simple. Because God was there as a witness when you spoke your marriage vows to your young bride, and now you've broken those vows, broken the faith-bond with your vowed companion, your covenant wife." We can also see that marriage covenants are established in the presence of God.

Blood was shed whenever covenants were established. In His consistency of design at creation, God made our bodies so that the covenant a man and wife enter is also established through the shedding of blood. It is a special event that binds God and the two people together for life. This is why virginity is a treasured thing in the law of God, as it is for many of today's generation, and why marriage is a covenant relationship between God and the man and woman as one entity. People who believe in the shedding of the divine blood of God through the body of Jesus Christ on the cross are covered by the Abrahamic covenant, in which God the Son was a party. This is confirmed in the following scriptures:
- "Just think how much more the blood of Christ will purify our consciences from sinful deeds so that we can worship the living God. For by the power of the eternal Spirit, Christ offered himself to God as a perfect sacrifice for our sins." Hebrews 9:14 (NLT)

- "His Son paid the price to free us, which means that our sins are forgiven." Colossians 1:14 (GW)
- "For everyone has sinned; we all fall short of God's glorious standard. Yet God, in his grace, freely makes us right in his sight. He did this through Christ Jesus when he freed us from the penalty for our sins." Romans 3:23-24 (NLT)
- "This means that anyone who belongs to Christ has become a new person. The old life is gone; a new life has begun! And all of this is a gift from God, who brought us back to himself through Christ. And God has given us this task of reconciling people to him. For God was in Christ, reconciling the world to himself, no longer counting people's sins against them. And he gave us this wonderful message of reconciliation." 2Corinthians 5:17-19 (NLT)

Therefore, with the changes that have been made by our creator on the inside of our hearts and with the newness that Jesus Christ gives us, we can still enter a love relationship with our spouse with a virgin's heart even though physically we may not be a virgin. With that newness in mind, one must spend time in careful thought and prayer about what is appropriate to share with one's partner as it pertains to any past sexual relationships. Obviously it is imperative to share with each other if those relationships existed, but as you have both been made new in Christ in spite of your sins, each couple must decide together how much they want to know about the details of those relationships. Know what to share and what to keep to yourself and pray

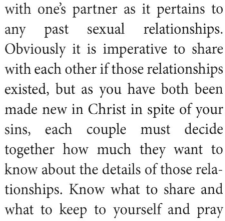

"we can still enter a love relationship with our spouse with a virgin's heart... though physically we may not be a virgin"

out, asking God to heal your mind and emotions. Some details might hurt your current relationship by inviting unwelcome thoughts and placing difficult images into your partner's head. After you decide what to share, you must also think and pray about how to share and when. Remember that some things are better prayed out rather than poured into your partner's ears.

Summary

1. Sexuality is connected to God's command to multiply and forms an emotional, intellectual and spiritual bond within the marriage.
2. A healthy sexual relationship starts with making yourself available to your spouse.
3. A kind and compatible relationship based on friendship is the foundation of an intimate sexual connection.
4. Valuing the life-long commitment of marriage lets your sexual relationship flourish, opening the way for true vulnerability and deepening passion.
5. There are five categories of important differences between male and female sexuality: attitude, stimulation, needs, sexual response and orgasm.
    - Men tend to be more physically oriented, while women are emotionally oriented.
    - Men are stimulated by the body, while women are more stimulated by the person.
    - Men need respect and admiration, while women need understanding and love.

7

God's Plan for Harmony

It is written in Psalm 133:1-3 (NIV): "How good and pleasant it is when God's people live together in unity! It is like precious oil… It is as if the dew… were falling. For there the Lord bestows his blessing, even life forevermore." David stated that harmony is pleasant and precious. Oil and dew as mentioned are symbolic of invigoration and renewal. Living in harmony by itself is pleasant and precious, and when God pours out His blessings, we experience "a part of heaven on earth." We must work toward maintaining harmony. With the absence of it there is great hardship, tension, division and the likelihood of divorce. Harmony is the principal factor in marriage because it helps us set the model that the next generation of our family is most likely to follow. Living in harmony does not mean that we will agree on everything, but we must agree on God's purpose for life. Our outward expression of harmony will reflect the inward condition of our heart.

A couple will start to experience harmony as they first accept their mates as a gift from God. God's gifts are always good, and they help us to be happy and fruitful and to fulfil the destiny of our lives. Genesis 2:18 (NIV) reads: "The Lord God said, "It is not good for the man to be alone. I will make a helper suitable for him." God did not create man to be on his own; he had greater plans for him, which he could not accomplish without the right relationships.

In addition to a relationship with God, which is most important, he needed to be in a personal, intimate relationship with a helper: a female human being. God made an incomparable gift for Adam. We see in Genesis 2:21-22 (NIV): "…the Lord God caused the man to fall into a deep sleep; and while he was sleeping, he took one of the man's ribs and … made a woman from the rib he had taken … and he brought her to the man."

When God made Eve, he weaved on the inside of her a unique creativity, potential and ability that is beyond the capacity of man, along with magnetism that man cannot resist or live comfortably or completely without. Adam was built with a unique need in him that could not be filled by the presence of God alone. It needed to be filled by the marriage relationship. Again this is easy to see in the text. God had said it is not good for the man to be alone, but in the Garden, Adam was not separated from God, so it is clear that he needed human contact. Not just any human contact either, because God did not create merely a friend for Adam. We are created to need the unique partnership provided by a godly marriage.

God Met Adam's Needs by Creating Eve

When God took the rib out of Adam to create Eve, Adam lost something that could only be found in Eve. The schools of psychology have discovered the right side of a man's brain functions differently from the right side of a woman. Coming together and acknowledging this fact will help couples increase harmony in marriage. Thus, in addition to creating Adam with a need for companionship that must be met by another human, God has added a layer of complexity by ensuring that Eve—and Eve, alone—can meet the need in Adam. This shows us something about how God views human marriage and how God wants us to treat our marriage partners. They are not replaceable. They are not people we choose lightly. Instead, our marriage partner is someone who helps us to find the truest version of ourselves.

> *"When God took the rib out of Adam to create Eve, Adam lost something that could only be found in Eve"*

The Pharisees came badgering Jesus on the subject of marriage relationships: "And he answering said to them, "Did ye not read, that He who made [them], from the beginning a male and a female made them, and said, For this cause shall a man leave father and mother, and cleave to his wife, and they shall be — the two —for one flesh? so that they are no more two, but one flesh; what therefore God did join together, let no man put asunder." Matthew 19:4-6 (YLT)

1. God fashioned Eve to be completely compatible with Adam. Again this shows us how God designed marriage. If a man and woman do not find everything they need inside their marriage, it is because they allow a void to be there by wrong thinking. We know this

because our marriage partners, like Eve for Adam, have been designed to be completely compatible with us.
2. Adam had the option to reject Eve, but he trusted God and accepted her. It was with the same free will that Adam and Eve later decided to taste the tree of knowledge. Adam could have chosen to ignore God's gift of Eve. However, trusting fully in God, Adam knew that someone God created for him would not be inferior to anyone or anything else.
3. We must accept our mates as a gift from God regardless of what we may see later. As we trust God, He will birth and develop qualities in our mates to make us complete and compatible with each other. In Genesis 2:23 (NIV), God illustrates the principle that must be a cornerstone of marriage: "The man said, 'This is now bone of my bones and flesh of my flesh; she shall be called "woman," for she was taken out of man.'" Therefore we must accept our mate as God's gift and trust in God's integrity. Adam enthusiastically received Eve because he knew and trusted God.

Like Adam, we as Christians need to trust God's design of our mate. We are compatible and complete for each other, regardless of the inevitable arguments and impediments that every marriage relationship will encounter. Rather than seek what we need from someone else, we must understand that God has equipped our mates with everything we need from a spouse and we must be content with the present good we are experiencing, as well as trust that God is at work to bring forth what may seem to be missing.

"Leaving and Cleaving" is the Responsibility of Both Parties

As discussed in Chapter 6, Genesis 2:24 (GW) reads: "That is why a man will leave his father and mother and be united with his wife, and they will become one flesh." Although this verse specifically calls for the man to leave his family, it goes on to talk of unity and becoming one flesh. How can a couple experience true unity without both parties "leaving and cleaving" together?

"It is the responsibility of both husband and wife to leave… family dynamics and cleave together… with God as their head—not their mother, father, brother or sister"

They cannot. "It is the responsibility of both husband and wife to leave' behind their old "family dynamics and cleave together" as one new family unit "with God as their head—not their mother, father, brother or sister'. Sometimes unfulfilled parents want to continue living their unfilled lives through their sons and daughters, but they will eventually contribute to the damage or destruction of their children's marriage. Having our perfect Heavenly Father as the head of your marriage, and not your imperfect parents or other people, can be of great gain and save you from much pain.

In order to become independent of your parents and build a new family unit together, the first step must be to leave your parents. However, this does not mean you should stop honouring your mother and father as commanded by God. Instead, you should strive to leave your parents and continue to honour them, bearing in mind your mate has now become the first priority in your life. Try to leave with the blessing of your parents. After all, our families can see our relationships in a way we cannot. If your parents do not approve of your relationship, you should view their disapproval from God's perspective, find out if their opinion is justified and most importantly address the issue God's way. In honouring them, you may need to give them an explanation of the decision you have made based on the premise that you want to please God first and then your mate. If you treat their concern in this matter, you are honouring them, honouring God above all, and showing respect for your mate. You should also strive to reconcile any differences or grievances you have with your parents before you leave. This includes any injuries inflicted by abuse in malfunctioning families and possibly your rebellion during your adolescent years.

Leaving your parents is not a time to decide that your concerns are important and theirs are inferior. It is a time to recognize any harm your malfunctioning family may have done or what you may have done, and seek forgiveness. Forgive and reconcile where necessary. However, this relationship cannot be built and cannot last if you hold onto childish ways and continue to hurt your parents, or if they are hurting you. For a harmonious marriage, you must do all you can according to biblical standards to maintain your relationship with your parents in a healthy manner. This will create a solid family foundation for future children. At this time, you must also beware of overdependence on, or co-dependence with, your parents for the following reasons:

- This is the biggest hindrance two people can face in experiencing harmony.
- Your mate and children can be hurt by such a problem for many generations.
- Unhealthy dependence will affect the intimacy and pleasure in your marital relationship.
- It can bring on depression, distrust and frustration in the marriage.
- When married, your accountability and priorities change.
- God remains your first priority in marriage; your mate becomes second and replaces your parents. After your

mate, your next priority should be your children; then come the parents, siblings and friends.

If you are discussing issues with parents, siblings or friends before you discuss them with your mate, there is already a problem. If you are spending more time with your parents and relatives than with your mate, you are giving the devil a foothold in your relationship and even "cheating" on your spouse. Couples should adapt to cultural changes, tolerate and participate in hobbies, and mature in faith together. Do devotions and pray together, share interests and opinions, and serve in church and community together. Invest in and try to add value to each other in whatever way possible.

God Uses Our Natural Differences to Build Harmony

Our natural differences are as cited in the Family Life Marriage Conference workbook:
- Gender
- Perspectives
- Temperament
- Background
- Preferences
- Roles

Our natural weaknesses are:
- Impatience
- Indecisiveness
- Disorganization
- A critical spirit
- Talkativeness
- Being demanding

We must do our part in complying with God's requirements for our roles and responsibilities in our marriage and trust Him to do His part to add harmony in our marriages. Always remember, it is not all up to God. We also have our part to play.

Summary

1. God says, in Genesis 2:18 (NIV): "It is not good for the man to be alone." Eve was created to fill this unique need in Adam that the presence of God alone couldn't satisfy; the husband and wife fill this need for each other in the same way.
2. You should accept your mate as a gift from God and trust God's design, even through inevitable arguments.
3. Both husband and wife should turn from their old family dynamics and come together to form a new family unit, independent of their parents.

8

The Husband's Role in Facilitating Harmony in Marriage

God created marriage for our benefit, but He also gave us responsibilities. It is important to follow the divine order of responsibilities He laid out in order to achieve true marital harmony. So that we better understand God's guidelines for a harmonious marriage, we will look at a few translations of specific scriptures:

God appointed the husband as the lead servant in the marital relationship and gave him responsibility for everything that needs to be done in the marriage. In the NIV version of Ephesians 5:23, the apostle Paul states, "For the husband is the head of the wife as Christ is the head of the church, his body, of which he is the Savior." Contrast this with The Message version of the same scripture: "The husband provides leadership to his wife the way Christ does to his church, not by domineering but by cherishing." Ephesians 5:23 (MSG) The two versions of this same scripture, side by side, shed light on exactly what God meant when He made the husband the head of the marriage relationship. When we think of Christ as the head of the church, we do not think of a man who issues commands or who demands devotion and submission. In the beginning, we were created as free moral beings with the option to choose the course of action we take in anything, whether it leads to life or death, blessings or curses. Nevertheless, as the son of God, co-creator of human beings and head of the church (the bridegroom), he modelled and inspired submission to God and devotion to His church (His bride). In the same way, the husband is the head of the marriage and should inspire submission and devotion by the way he relates to his wife: with love, respect, sensitivity, caring and an attitude of humility. If a man serves his wife sacrificially and unconditionally, he will naturally emerge as the head of their relationship: not as the master, but as another servant, joined together with his wife.

"the husband… the lead servant… not by domineering but by cherishing"

In turn, God appointed the wife to be the helper or co-worker in the relationship. Wives, do not let your preconceived notions dictate the way you think of the role of helper. The helper in the marriage is an absolutely vital role. After all, a head without a body cannot accomplish anything. In Genesis we read: The Lord God said, "It is not good for the man to be alone. I will make a helper suitable for him." Genesis 2:18 (NIV) Compare this to the NLT version of the same verse: Then the Lord God said, "It is not good for man to be alone. I will make a helper who is just right for him." As above, these two translations give further insight into God's plans for wives in the marriage relationship.

In the previous chapter, we learned that man was not created to be alone and that Eve was created specifically for him. Here we can see again that man needed a wife to be complete. We can also see that he needed someone who would function as his helper and not try to be the head as some wives try to be. However, he did not need just any helper. He needed a helper who would be just right for him. The wife's role in the relationship is just as important as the husband's role. God has designed husbands and wives in such a manner that they add value to each other, but that can only happen if they do their part in taking advantage of that divine opportunity. It will come to pass as husbands first take the lead and function as God created them to be. You can see more of this intended relationship in 1 Corinthians 11:11 (ISV): "In the Lord, however, woman is not independent of man, nor is man independent of woman." This shows definitively that husband and wife are designed to complete each other in what is meant to be an interdependent marriage relationship.

It is also clear from the Bible that husband and wife were designed by God to have equal value in the relationship, as shown in Galatians 3:28 (NIV): "… nor is there male and female, for you are all one in Christ Jesus." Again The Message version can give us further clarity on this passage: "In Christ's family there can be no division into … male and female. Among us you are all equal. That is, we are all in a common relationship with Jesus Christ." It is our worth in Christ that matters most and His view of us that should form our lives here on earth. In Christ, man and woman are equal. Don't forget husbands and wives are both imperfect humans whose minds and bodies contain residues of the Adamic nature, but in the dimension of our recreated, born-again spirit, we are perfect. Therefore neither is any better than the other or more important. So that is how we should see and relate to each other in our relationship.

In that same breath, God has designed husband and wife in such a way that they are only able to fulfil their roles in the marriage through their dependence on His power, which works from within them as they maintain a relationship and remain connected to Him. Jesus himself affirms this in The Message version of John 15:5: "I am the Vine, you are the branches. When you're joined with me and I with you, the relation intimate and organic, the harvest is sure to be abundant. Separated, you can't produce a thing." In the NIV, this verse ends with the words: "apart from me you can do nothing." What this phrase means is that, apart from Him, we will accomplish nothing inspired or empowered by Him. Therefore, in the long run, if we do not continue to remain in Him, our compromise will surely invite corruption. If we have been told by God that we can do "nothing" in our lives, then marriage is no different. We will only produce lasting and acceptable fruitfulness in our marriages if Christ is in the centre of our lives.

There are two important concepts contained in the Bible that are essential for men to understand and implement in their marriage relationships. First, husbands must love as Christ did. Secondly, husbands must lead like a servant.

Love as Christ Did

In Ephesians 5:25 (MSG), we read: "Husbands, go all out in love for your wives, exactly as Christ did for the church—a love marked by giving, not getting." Love is seeking God's best for our spouse. It is based on an act of will on our part, not passive feelings or a reactive attitude. Colossians 3:19 (MSG) says: "Husbands, go all out in love for your wives. Don't take advantage of them." Likewise, this same verse in NIV says: "Husbands, love your wives and do not be harsh with them." Thus, we love our wives as God loves through our kind words and thoughts, along with sacrificial actions. It is not enough to have good intentions without follow-through. We must be willing to deny ourselves and strive to be obedient to the role God has designed for us, not only acting because we expect something in return. When we decide to be the person God wants us to be, we will find that we are naturally more sensitive and genuinely loving, not prone to manipulate situations for our own gratification. Love allows us to build each other up. The love we show to our wife will allow her to have a healthy self-image and the confidence to know that we can be relied upon. A loving husband will help his wife spiritually and emotionally, as well as through actions, and he will allow her to develop in every aspect of her life to reach the full potential that God has given her. Ephesians 5:28-29 (NIV) says: "…husbands ought to love their wives as their own bodies. He who loves his wife loves himself. After all, no one ever hated their own body, but they feed and care for their body…" Similarly, the same verses in The Message say, "And that is how husbands ought to love their wives. They're really doing themselves a favour—since they're already 'one' in marriage. No one abuses his own body, does he? No, he feeds and pampers it."

Lead Like a Servant

In a marriage relationship, the chain of authority runs first from Christ to the husband, then from the husband to the wife. The authority of Christ is the authority of God. All links in the chain must submit to authority; if anyone breaks rank, then we risk failure. In John 13, Jesus shows His disciples the example of leadership in all areas of life. Definitely this example is for husbands to lead in their marriage also. He demonstrated the full extent of true love, humility and selflessness, and a willingness to go all the way to serve to the end of one's life by washing the disciples' feet close to the end of His life. He broke the traditions of leaders of that age as well as the current. He got up from the meal and stripped himself down to the attire, took off his outer clothing, left with his tunic, a shorter garment. He tied a towel around his waist with which to dry their feet. Obviously, this is not what one would expect a master, rabbi or teacher to do. He knew that Judas, His betrayer, and Peter, who disowned Him, as well as doubting Thomas, were there. Nevertheless in humility He served them as a slave. After Jesus finished washing their feet, he replaced his outer garments, returned to his seat, and asked, "Do you understand what I have done for you?" John 13:12 (NIV) While in their embarrassed amazement, Jesus summoned them to practise this concept of servant leadership in whatever office of leadership they would find themselves: "Now that I, your Lord and Teacher, have washed your feet, you also should wash one another's feet. I have set you an example that you should do as I have done for you." John 13:14-15 (NIV) Jesus did not necessarily mean that they should literally go wash feet, but apply the concept in going all the way is practising servanthood.

The example of Christ frees us from our traditions and from modern society's norms to be the leader He has designed us to be. In Mark 10:42-43 (NIV), we read: "Jesus called them together and said, 'You know that those who are regarded as rulers of the Gentiles lord it over them, and their high officials exercise authority over them. Not so with you. Instead, whoever wants to become great among you must be your servant.'" The Message version of these verses provides a slightly different take: "Jesus got them together to settle things down. 'You've observed how godless rulers throw their weight around,' he said, 'and when people get a little power how quickly it goes to their heads. It's not going to be that way with you. Whoever wants to be great must become a servant.'" Christ displayed leadership through servant functions. He showed that leaders should have a servant's heart, be humble enough to break traditions of religion and trends of society, and do whatever is needed—even if it may seem to be the lowest function in the process of serving. He commanded us to embrace that concept, and in practice, this might include a willingness to carry out such tasks as cleaning the house, doing laundry, washing dishes and yes, even washing your wife's feet if she would like you to.

Husband's Leadership and Responsibility in the Home

Leadership involves providing and facilitating growth and development in the spirit, mind and physical body. "But if any provide not for his own, and specially for those of his own house, he hath denied the faith, and is worse than an infidel." 1 Tim 5:8 (KJV) In leading, a husband should be the priest of his home. He should have daily devotions and/or Bible study and get his family involved in a working relationship with a healthy church that provides an opportunity for each member to be ministered to, as well as for them to serve in the capacity of their divine gifted potential. He should help his wife and children to discover and develop their talents and ministry gifts, mature in their identity, and keep healthy. It is also his responsibility is to provide physically, that is food, clothing and shelter, etc. In today's society, however, most wifes will often willingly help with this.

Leadership in Marriage Should Be Sensitive, Caring and Gentle

Authority should not be abused. A husband must remember his wife may be weaker in certain areas. Still, she may be stronger in others. To lead means to show the way and take the initiative, and a woman who reveres God will follow. Do not push or pull too hard because this can bring frustration, stress and disharmony. Remain caring and sharing. Husbands, do not abandon your roles as priest, provider and protector. The fulfilment of the husband's role in marriage, as defined by God, leads to harmony. Malachi 2:15-17 (MSG) states:

> God, not you, made marriage. His Spirit inhabits even the smallest details of marriage. And what does he want from marriage? Children of God, that's what. So guard the spirit of marriage within you. Don't cheat on your spouse.
>
> "I hate divorce," says the God of Israel. God-of-the-Angel-Armies says, "I hate the violent dismembering of the 'one flesh' of marriage." So watch yourselves. Don't let your guard down. Don't cheat.
>
> You make God tired with all your talk.
>
> "How do we tire him out?" you ask.
>
> By saying, "God loves sinners and sin alike. God loves all." And also by saying, "Judgment? God's too nice to judge."

Summary

1. Men are to accept God's design for marriage.
2. Men are to love their wives the way Christ loves the church.
3. Men are to accept their responsibility to lead as Christ led, and as the Bible instructs them.
4. Men are to seek to understand their wives, attempt to meet their needs in loving ways, and lead them with credibility and integrity. This will inspire wives to highly esteem their husbands.
5. Men are to remember that God has designed a husband and wife to fulfil His design through dependence on Him and on each other.
6. As a husband commits himself to God's design for marriage, he will be strengthened with humility and

wisdom to demonstrate the love and respect a man needs to become the servant-leader God has called him to be.

9

The Wife's Role in Facilitating Harmony in Marriage

As the helper in the marriage, a wife has a few specific responsibilities that will, if she executes them properly, contribute to a healthy and harmonious marriage. First, it is important that the wife accept God's design for marriage. Through discernment and remembering how God designed the marriage relationship, it is easy to understand God's designs for marriage and therefore to accept and practise them, particularly if the wife is a believer.

In his letter to the Ephesians, Paul tells us that a wise woman walks with discernment and knows that God's ways are most important and are genuine principles for a healthy and harmonious marriage. She will be careful how she chooses to live her life: "So then, be very careful how you live. Don't live like foolish people but like wise people. Make the most of your opportunities because these are evil days." Ephesians 5:15-16 (GW) Remember that part of God's design is that husband and wife have equal value. Therefore it is of vital importance to harmony that each party diligently practise their roles and realize in doing so they are honouring God. In Galatians 3:28 (MSG), Paul writes: "In Christ's family there can be no division into …male and female. Among us you are all equal. That is, we are all in a common relationship with Jesus Christ." Just as God has designed men and women to have equal value in the marriage relationship, He has also designed them to be interdependent, as two hands each helping to wash the other. This is made obvious in 1 Corinthians 11:11-12 (NLT): "But among the Lord's people, women are not independent of men, and men are not independent of women. For although the first woman came from man, every other man was born from a woman, and everything comes from God." With God's help, a wise woman can take these elements and discover His divine order of responsibility in marriage. For the wife, this means:

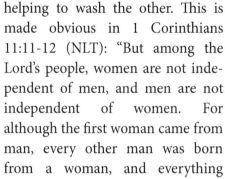

"men and women to have equal value in the marriage relationship"

1. To support and help rather than to exercise superiority, be controlling or attempt to manipulate her husband, or act on evil influences as Eve did in the Garden of Eden.
2. To understand that although God has designated the husband as the general manager, he can only function well with a chief administrator and good support staff.
3. To understand that God has designated the wife as the helper, not a replica or carbon copy of her husband. She is meant to complement and as a servant helper to assist her husband in accomplishing his duties. In Genesis 2:18 (MSG), God said: "It's not good for the Man to be alone; I'll make him a helper, a companion."
4. To know that she can and will fulfil His design through dependence on His guidance and power: "I am the

vine; you are the branches. If you remain in me and I in you, you will bear much fruit; apart from me you can do nothing." John 15:5 (NIV)

After a wife has accepted God's design for marriage, she has other important responsibilities to remember. These include loving, supporting and respecting her husband.

Loving Your Husband

Titus 2:4 (NLT) states: "…train the younger women to love their husbands…" To love your husbands in the way a godly marriage requires, wives must first understand what love really is. The true meaning of godly love includes:

1. Accepting your husband as he is, an imperfect person. Wives must be willing to love him unconditionally based on the value that he has as God's gift to them, and not only accept him when you think he is doing or acting as he should.

    "Accepting your husband as he is, an imperfect person… Supporting him through failures"

2. Understanding his way of thinking and helping him when possible. All of us are challenged with negative and evil thoughts frequently and also experience temptations or negative feelings. Rather than trying to change your husband's thoughts/feelings or persuading him to hide the negative ones, you should embrace him even in his imperfections, as he embraces you even in yours. Helping him to work through and deal

with the negative ones is not only an act of love, but it also will make your marriage much better.
3. Supporting him through failures and times when he feels defeated. Think for a moment about how you would like your husband to act in the wake of your own personal failures or defeats. You would hope for his support and love, not for him to say "I told you so" or to explain to you just how wrong you were. So give him that same gift and help him to rebuild his confidence with the knowledge that you are always there for him. Do not criticize, condemn, nag or compare him with other women's husbands. This behaviour emasculates him and corrupts his potential and self-image.

If we truly love each other, we will make sacrifices for each other. Making your husband a priority, particularly in the following ways, is essential:

Listen to him, talk with him and encourage him in his wholesome pursuits.

Spend time with him and keep some of your energy for him. Try not to overcommit yourself outside of the marriage and only give your husband what you have left. Make your plans and commitments the other way around instead, giving your time and energy to your marriage ahead of other pursuits. In doing so, you are facilitating harmony and investing in your children and grandchildren.

Provide your husband with physical attention, as discussed earlier in Song of Songs 7:10-13 (NIV):

> I belong to my beloved…
> Come, my beloved, let us go to the countryside,
> let us spend the night in the villages.
> Let us go early to the vineyards
> to see if the vines have budded,

> if their blossoms have opened,
> and if the pomegranates are in bloom–
> there I will give you my love.
> The mandrakes send out their fragrance,
> and at our door is every delicacy,
> both new and old,
> that I have stored up for you, my beloved.

These verses make the point clearly. The wife is inviting her husband to spend quality time together, in the night and in the morning, at both the end of the day and at the beginning. Any different approach has proven to drive spouses apart and bring discord.

Encouraging Your Husband

Proverbs 31:10-12 (NIV) says: "A wife of noble character who can find? She is worth far more than rubies. Her husband has full confidence in her and lacks nothing of value. She brings him good, not harm, all the days of her life." Take note that this verse says a wife of "noble character," not just a wife. The word "noble" means righteous, gracious and decent. Righteousness is drawn from a relationship with The Righteous One and supported by people who provide righteous influence. When you encourage and support your husband, you complete the marital relationship. You cannot be competitive in your marriage. The book of Proverbs is full of excellent advice for wives:

Better to live alone in a tumbledown shack than share a mansion with a nagging spouse. Proverbs 21:9 (MSG)

A worthy wife is a crown for her husband, but a disgraceful woman is like cancer in his bones. The plans of the godly are just; the advice of the wicked is treacherous. Proverbs 12:4-5 (NLT)

Wives must support and encourage their husbands rather than make demands, criticize condemn or compare them. A husband needs his wife's support in every area, from his job or business to the daily life in the home and his involvement in the church. He is the leader in the relationship and the wife's support is vital to keeping that relationship strong and healthy. In the scriptures, God calls this support "submission," and it is the key ingredient in a harmonious marriage. In Ephesians 5:21-23 (NIV), Paul writes: "Submit to one another out of reverence for Christ. Wives, submit yourselves to your own husbands as you do to the Lord. For the husband is the head of the wife as Christ is the head of the church, his body, of which he is the Saviour." The word "submit" does not mean that you are inferior or less intelligent, or that you will lose your identity. Submission in the biblical sense is not blind obedience. It is a form of surrender. It is giving yourself over to the relationship and accepting that instead of thinking of yourself, you are now in all things working to be united with your husband. You are not alone in being called to submission, though. The phrase, "submit to one another" is very clear: it means both mates have to submit to each other. Both husband and wife are to submit to each other after considering God's set of rules for the behaviour of males and females in the marriage relationship.

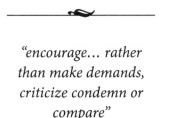

"encourage… rather than make demands, criticize condemn or compare"

After telling both husband and wife to submit to each other, Paul then turns his attention to the wife specifically, saying, "Submit to your husbands as to the Lord." Ephesians 5:22 (NLT) As a wife, it is important to understand that this is not an exhortation, but a command. It is not something that can be either adhered to or ignored based on your feelings. It is something God commands of you as a wife. What does that look like in your daily life? First, your husband must be following after God's heart. Then, when a decision needs to be made, there must be diligent dialogue between you and your husband in relation to the issue at hand. An educated decision must be made, so if professional or spiritual wisdom is needed, you should consult the appropriate outside authorities. Following all of those steps, if you and your husband do not come to an agreement, then you must submit to your husband's decision. Make it clear that you disagree, but submit to his leadership. Titus 2:5 (NLT) says: "to live wisely and be pure, to work in their homes, to do good, and to be submissive to their husbands. Then they will not bring shame on the word of God."

In modern life, we often misunderstand submission. Submission does not imply that the wife is of lesser value in the relationship or that she must follow her husband in blind obedience. Men and women are of equal value in the sight of God, and each person has a special identity as someone God has created and loves. Instead submission means the wife is willing to respond to her husband in a way that will respect God's design for marriage. This benefits both spouses, as well as the children who are our heritage. Just as we anticipate that the husband will submit to God and love his wife, we expect that the wife would submit to the husband and respect him. This would include respectfully sharing your own opinions, wisdom and knowledge so that the family unit will prosper. The wife can do much to empower her husband to lead and follow after God's will for their lives. However, submission on the part of the wife definitely does not give the husband the power to violate any laws. No wife must submit to a husband's physical or emotional abusive, either of herself or their children. She must not submit to her husband's actions if he fails to follow the laws of the country they live in.

Respecting Your Husband

Ephesians 5:33 (AMPC) states: "…and let the wife see that she respects and reverences her husband [that she notices him, regards him, honours him, prefers him, venerates, and esteems him; and that she defers to him, praises him, and loves and admires him exceedingly]." If a wife truly respects her husband, she will treat him with special consideration, and try to understand and appreciate him even though he is not a perfect person. She will consider the challenges he faces as he accepts responsibility for the leadership of the family, and she will see the pressures that he may be experiencing in his role. She will accept that he, as a man, is different from who she is as a woman. A man can thrive more easily—and he can even make better decisions—when he feels he has his wife's respect. It is good for a wife to express that respect, as well as the trust and confidence she has in her husband. Special words and actions can also help to show him he is respected. She can be look for ways to assist him and encourage him when he appears to have a need. Praise and admiration can also let him know that he is respected. Most people like to hear when they have done a job well, but it can be just as important to let him know that even when he fails at something, the wife remains proud of who he is and all of the effort that he makes to accomplish tasks and also to become the person he desires to be.

Summary

As a wife, you help to bring harmony to the marital relationship when you actively love, encourage and respect your husband. In closing this chapter, I would like you to consider two wives mentioned in the Bible. First, think of Job's first wife—whose name was never mentioned in the Bible—yet she may be considered the most despicable woman in the Bible. If we knew her name, it would take its place in the Hall of Shame with the likes of Jezebel, Delilah and Michal. Because of her worldly ways, she experienced the agony of watching her children suffer and die, and she experienced dramatic financial loss. In one terrible day, she lost everything she had. She found herself not only bankrupt, but also homeless and forced to beg outside the city dump. She became a caretaker for her disease-ravaged husband and eventually told him to curse God and die. Yet God restored Job with a new family.

In contrast, consider Abraham's wife, Sarah. Abraham was a man of faith, but also of fear, and in his fear he disobeyed God and worse. In a truly heinous act, he gave Sarah away in order to save himself. In all of his disobedience, Sarah obeyed and submitted to him. She was described as a Proverbs 31 woman, and Peter referred to her as a woman of faith and confidence, recommending her as a model to all women. Though she was hot-tempered and strong-willed, she never disobeyed her husband. Instead she called him Lord, followed him through the desert, and experienced great peril as a result. However, in the end, she also experienced prosperity and the good will of the Lord. Her name is recorded in the Bible and eternal halls of fame.

10

Blended Families

If you are heading toward re-marriage or are already in another marriage, you will surely need to address the blending of two families. This can happen for at least a couple of reasons: divorce or death. In both cases, it is a delicate situation that must be handled with greater wisdom and sensitivity than a nuclear family in order to ensure a harmonious and sound marriage. Half of all families today are blended families, and unfortunately, according to the website successfulstepfamilies.com, the divorce rate for second marriages when only one partner has children is over 65 per cent, but when both partners have children, the rate rises to 70 per cent, primarily due to a lack of understanding of how to address the challenges with which these families are faced. As I said in Chapter 1, one of God's purposes for marriage is multiplying and leaving a godly legacy, so it is imperative that

"Your children will need acceptance, assurance, safety and freedom from guilt and shame"

children in blended families be made to feel loved, understood and welcomed. In this way, parents who introduce children from previous marriages into one family can and should continue live out God's purpose for their marriage.

Before you even consider a remarriage, you must first make sure that you and your possible future partner have discussed your values, beliefs and religion. Don't just stop with having a conversation, though. Make sure you are both in agreement. Putting off disagreements on these main issues will only invite discord into your new family. Additionally, you must openly discuss your family histories with each other. Any sicknesses, addictions, liabilities, criminal records, prior relationships and other baggage must be disclosed and addressed, not only for the two new spouses, but the children as well. You both have to accept each other's children as your own, with unconditional love. Your children will need acceptance, assurance, safety and freedom from guilt and shame, issues with which children in blended families struggle. They need, in a greater way, stable families with parents of integrity and single-mindedness in their approach to life. They need the freedom to develop in all of life's stages, to make mistakes, to slip and sometimes fall, and most importantly, the opportunity to rise again. They will definitely need to have both of you there to lovingly help them mature gracefully into adults.

It is important for couples heading into a remarriage after a divorce to take part in re-marital counselling before saying "I do" again. Because you may have already experienced one or probably more broken relationships, you need counselling and/or therapy to make sure that you don't carry the baggage from your first marriage and or second into your next. You will learn how to avoid making the same mistakes a second time and how to make sure your relationship is solid before taking the major step of marrying again. Blending your families can be successful, as can your new marriage, as long as you start out with good guidance and follow a well thought-out plan.

You must be prepared to challenge the status quo victoriously, with the necessary insight and wisdom, in order to bring about harmony in blending your two families, because it is one of the most challenging kinds of mergers faced by humanity since the beginning of time. It is very easy for almost every member of the family to end up hurt, sad, mad or all three. After a divorce or early death, most people choose to remarry at some point in the course of their lives, which necessarily means any children they have will become part of a new, unfamiliar family unit. The negative effects of a badly managed union can follow your family for generations to come. The damages that can come from blending a family are obvious in the Bible in the story of Joseph. Joseph was one of Jacob's many children by four different women. As the son of Jacob's preferred wife Rachel, Joseph was obviously Jacob's favourite. The obviousness of Jacob's preference led to a strong dislike of Joseph and eventually the plot conceived by his brothers to remove him from their lives completely. In their anger and hatred, they first decided to kill him, then change their minds and simply throw him in a pit, and finally chose to sell him as a slave. In the end, all of this worked to God's plan and for Joseph's good, but the seeds of discord were sown by Joseph's parents, not by his own choices. If, in blending your families, either spouse shows greater concern or love for one child (or set of children) over the other, similar anger will arise among your children.

Before you begin the formal process of bringing two families together, either by marrying or living together, the children from both sides of the relationship should be given time to get to know each other and establish a friendship. You will need to make

"make sure the children are compatible before you become one family"

sure the children are compatible before you become one family. Your families should also be fully established in a good relationship before any other steps are taken to live together. If you find that your children aren't compatible, your marriage or blended living arrangements should be delayed as long as necessary, and even ruled out if there is no way to bring your children together. Remember that marriage is about family, and if you force your children into a family unit that they are not ready for or compatible with, you will do damage to your children and your new marriage. Once you have decided to bring the families together, all of the children should see their new home before moving in. They should see the rooms they will be sleeping in, and if you are moving into a house one of you already owns, they should see the efforts you have already made to make it feel like their home as well as yours.

Trying to bring two families together after divorce is even more difficult. This is one of the reasons God hates divorce, as decreed in Malachi 2:16 (NLT): "For I hate divorce! says the Lord, the God of Israel." Notice that it is the act of divorce God hates and not the broken people who get divorced. The destruction that follows divorce is what is hurtful to His heart and hateful to Him. To avoid that destruction and ensure that your blended families live in peace, you must put a plan in place before your marriage. Each member of your new family—your children, your spouse and you—will enter this time of life with their own baggage. Examine each person's baggage closely and make a plan for how you will both accept the baggage every person has and help them to heal from it eventually. It will take time, patience, compassion, compromise, godly wisdom and personal, intimate relationships with all involved to first accomplish and then maintain harmony. The roles and responsibilities of each spouse must be agreed upon, including for tasks such as budgeting and domestic issues such as chores. Two important things you must make sure to cover in your plan are discipline and time spent with children.

Discipline

Every child needs discipline for many reasons. In disciplining children, parents need to be first friendly, then fair and finally, firm—still never failing to compromise to some extent. Discipline lets children know they are loved, helps them to understand boundaries, and helps them to grow up respecting and honouring God and others. For children of blended families, discipline can be difficult. Two parents who have not been raising children together will be doing so now, and their different established styles can clash or be at odds. Children must know, from the start, that their two parents are of one accord as far as rules and boundaries are concerned. They also should know what consequences to expect if they do not live up to expectations, particularly if the consequences are changed from their original family unit.

"Children must know, from the start, that their two parents are of one accord"

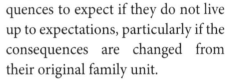

You must present a unified front as two spouses and not allow your different parenting styles to become obvious to your children. Never blame your spouse or let your child believe that you would choose to discipline him or her differently. This will cause resentment. Most importantly, if both spouses have children they are bringing into the new marriage, it is imperative that you never have double standards when disciplining your children. You must be consistent at all times, so that no child feels less loved or left out of the new family unit.

Furthermore, your plan for discipline must include your ex-spouse if you are divorced. Having different expectations and consequences in different households can be both confusing and frustrating for your children, no matter their age. It is your job to make their transition as smooth as possible by maintaining a cordial relationship with your ex and by including him or her in your plans for discipline. In some cases, even if you and your current spouse make it clear that you are united in your own home, the presence of another parent who disagrees with your strategies can damage your hard work. If you need help in this matter, you should contact your pastor or a qualified Christian family counsellor. Once all the parents are in agreement about discipline, the child should be disciplined lovingly by preferable the biological parent.

Time Spent Together

As you take two separate families and make them one, an easily overlooked, but very important aspect of relationship building is the time you spend together. This means time together as an entire family unit, as well as one-on-one time between parents and their natural children as well as step-parents and their new step-children. It is important for your children to see your entire family as one unit, but it is equally important for them to feel loved by the new parent in their lives while maintaining the special bond they have already with their natural parent. None of these relationships can be ignored or left to chance if you want to successfully create a new family unit. Be sure to show love and appreciation for each child in your family based on his or her unique characteristics. Make note of the ways in which each child gives and receives love, and go out of your way to show them love in the ways they best understand. Express joy, celebrate their accomplishments, and do not fall short in comforting them in their failures. Strive to connect with your children in ways that will have special meaning and make them feel loved and secure.

The time you spend together should also help your children, both biological and new, cope with the changes in their lives. This includes going from whatever family structure they had before to the new one. It also includes changes in everyday life from what school they attend, to moving into a new house or neighbourhood, and even down to what food they eat. These things may seem simple to you, but in the context of a new family, even small changes in routine can feel monumental to a child. Be sure to take extra time to help your children make any transitions they may need to between parents' houses, for instance, if they stay with one family on weekends and one during the week. This is a complicated prospect for many children, and they will need extra help from both their natural parents and their new step-parents to feel comfortable.

If both you and your spouse have children from a previous marriage, the bonding between kids is just as important as the bonding between child and step-parents. Help your children to find shared interests and activities so they have a solid foundation for their new sibling relationships. Make sure, at the same time, to allow them time and space when they need it—in many cases, children will naturally bond with another family quickly, but it is imperative to respect their occasional need to retreat to the sibling boundaries they have known their whole lives, so they do not feel forced. Love and affection take time to grow. Help the process to occur naturally, without rushing or demanding more from children than they are capable of giving. Remember, after all, that they are still children! Friendship must first be developed with your step-children. Following that, fairness must be practised, and children should not be expected to conform to the same levels of maturity and adaptability as an adult. Finally, exercise a firmness they can respect and rely on, always maintaining a

"Remember... they are still children! Friendship must first... Following that, fairness... Finally... firmness... always maintaining a level of compromise"

level of compromise that all adults have agreed upon. In this way, though it will likely be difficult, you can successfully blend two families into one, and your children can reap the benefits of your hard work for the rest of their lives, and even for generations to follow.

Summary

Many blended families end in divorce because they don't understand the challenges they will face. There are steps you can take to make sure all children in a blended family feel equally loved.
1. Discuss all baggage from past relationships with your future spouse to avoid future confrontation that could make a child feel ashamed or guilty.
2. Take part in re-marital counselling to avoid the mistakes that affected the first marriage.
3. Give all of the children time to become friends before starting the formal blending process.
4. Both partners should agree on a plan for tasks like chores, budgeting and discipline of children, as well as making sure equal time is spent with all of them.
5. With due diligence and God's grace appropriate a blended family can be harmonious.

11

Money Management and Budgeting

"Don't Allow the Tail to Wag the Dog"
(cited in McGraw-Hill's Dictionary of American Idioms and Phrasal Verbs)

Before David and Grace got married, they spent time in premarital counselling to make sure they were compatible and ready. Importantly, the counselling covered money management among the other topics, so they learned that there were a few crucial steps to take if they wanted harmony in their marriage as far as money was concerned. Before the wedding, they knew they would need to join their bank accounts and have a budget plan in place before they spent a dime as a married couple. Immediately after returning from their honeymoon, they implemented everything they had learned. With gross earnings of $8,000/month, they started following their budgeted plan. Ten per cent of the money went straight back to God in the form of a tithe. Of the rest, 10 per cent went into savings, 70 per cent was allocated to living expenses, and the other 20 per cent went toward debt repayment. The living expenses category allowed each some spending money—Grace getting $100 every month and David getting $75. With the plan in place and being followed, their money was managed and rather than causing them problems, it added to the harmony of their union and financial success

Abigail and Harry, unfortunately, had a very a different experience. Without any pre-marital counselling, Abigail and Harry decided to keep separate bank accounts, as they were accustomed to doing as a dating couple. Even though they started out with more money than David and Grace had every month—gross earnings of $12,000/month—every financial decision was made independently. David's expenses were his and Grace's expenses were hers. Instead of bringing them together, money drove them apart and made their marriage combative. Even though they had more than enough, financial conversations always revolved around who owed whom money or whose job it was to pay a specific bill. So instead of harmony, they experienced havoc in their relationship, financial disaster and their marriage did not end well.

God wants us, as His children, to use His wisdom in managing our finances, to be masters of our money instead of letting our money master us. The misuse, abuse and/or mismanagement of money is the root of so many of humanity's problems: individual tensions, family conflicts, interpersonal strife, anger and more.

> **"Money in most cases is not the problem, but the person who spends it has the problem."**
>
> *(Gary R. Collins)*

It is no surprise then, that money becomes an issue in many marriages today. So as you prepare for a harmonious and godly union, it is necessary to discuss how money will be managed in your marriage and to carefully decide on a financial plan. The first thing couples must understand is that the Bible is often misquoted on the subject of money. Many people say that money is the root of all evil, when in fact Paul specified that it is the love of money that leads to evil. Money itself is a necessary part of life, provided to us by God who supplies us with enough to meet our needs. It is when we spend our money on things we don't need that we find ourselves burdened by financial problems. God expects us to be good stewards of everything provided for us, including money. He requires that we manage our finances wisely, balancing our budgets by considering our income and expenses in all of the areas where we spend. This includes both the essentials for living such as housing, clothing, food and transportation, as well as those areas we all spend in that help us to live happier and more comfortable lives, such as vacations, hobbies, entertainment, cosmetics and gifts.

No success happens without a good plan, and having a good budget plan for all of the above and whatever else is important to you and your spouse is crucial. Without a plan, failure will follow. It is written in Proverbs 29:18 (KJV): "Where there is no vision the people perish." Along with the other visions people have for their lives, they should have a vision for their finances. Jesus said in Luke 14:28-29 (NASB): "For which one of you, when he wants to build a tower, does not first sit down and calculate the cost to see if he has enough to complete it? Otherwise, when he has laid a foundation and is not able to finish, all who observe it begin to ridicule him." Since no one wants to fail, it is necessary to approach financial planning in a business-like manner with sensibility and systematic diligence. God calls us to be disciplined people. We must handle our income with godly

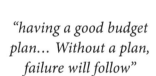

"having a good budget plan... Without a plan, failure will follow"

wisdom and only then can we expect to be the long-lasting masters of our finances.

It is possible for irresponsible or foolish spending to be the outward symptom of inner problems. Marital problems, mental problems, physical problems, burnout or spiritual brokenness can all subconsciously contribute to out-of-control spending. In these cases, it is essential to discover and deal with the underlying problem. This issue may need intervention in the form of a Christian counsellor. We are warned, too, to be wary of the perils of money, particularly the pursuit of wealth for wealth's sake, as discussed in 1 Timothy 6:6-11 (NIV): "But godliness with contentment is great gain …. if we have food and clothing, we will be content with that. Those who want to get rich fall into temptation and a trap and into many foolish and harmful desires that plunge people into ruin and destruction…. Some people… pierced themselves with many griefs. But you, man of God, flee from all this…"

Money management was taught by Jesus to his followers in the parable of the talents, which reads as follows in Matthew 25:14-29 (GW):

> "The kingdom of heaven is like a man going on a trip. He called his servants and entrusted some money to them. He gave one man ten thousand dollars, another four thousand dollars, and another two thousand dollars. Each was given money based on his ability. Then the man went on his trip.
>
> "The one who received ten thousand dollars invested the money at once and doubled his money. The one who had four thousand dollars did the same and also doubled his money. But the one who received two thousand dollars went off, dug a hole in the ground, and hid his master's money.

"After a long time, the master of those servants returned and settled accounts with them. The one who received ten thousand dollars brought the additional ten thousand. He said, 'Sir, you gave me ten thousand dollars. I've doubled the amount.'

"His master replied, 'Good job! You're a good and faithful servant! You proved that you could be trusted with a small amount. I will put you in charge of a large amount. Come and share your master's happiness.'

"The one who received four thousand dollars came and said, 'Sir, you gave me four thousand dollars. I've doubled the amount.'

"His master replied, 'Good job! You're a good and faithful servant! You proved that you could be trusted with a small amount. I will put you in charge of a large amount. Come and share your master's happiness.'

"Then the one who received two thousand dollars came and said, 'Sir, I knew that you are a hard person to please. You harvest where you haven't planted and gather where you haven't scattered any seeds. I was afraid. So I hid your two thousand dollars in the ground. Here's your money!'

"His master responded, 'You evil and lazy servant! If you knew that I harvest where I haven't planted and gather where I haven't scattered, then you should have invested my money with the bankers. When I returned, I would have received my money back with interest. Take the two thousand dollars away from him! Give it to the one who has the ten thousand!'

"To all who have, more will be given, and they will have more than enough. But everything will be taken away from those who don't have much."

In the above, Jesus warns exactly how mismanagement of resources can affect people. In the end, the unfaithful servant is alienated from his friends and loses what little he was given to begin with. Kenneth M. Miller drew a number of foundational financial management principles from Jesus' teachings in the parable of the talents, from which we can all learn, namely:
1. God entrusts resources to us in many forms.
2. God gives the resources to different people (families) in different amounts.
3. God expects us to manage our resources and plan with the goal of making a profit.
4. God condemns laziness and anxiety in planning, which we know from the harsh rebuke given to the do-nothing manager.
5. God holds each manager equally accountable even though some have more resources than others.
6. God's word and will for our lives are hindered if we don't manage our finances well.
7. We can be humiliated if we do not humble ourselves in our stewardship and allow ourselves to grow and learn how to manage our resources.

In order to manage our money wisely, we must first learn some truths about wise money management. A few important ones are:
1. Gain honestly: do not attempt "get rich quick" schemes.
2. Spend and invest carefully with the guidance of professionals.
3. Spend realistically. Keep your heart content where material goods are concerned and stay out of debt when possible. If you must go into debt, have a plan for repayment that you know you can follow through on. The Bible gives little leeway in sanctioning credit card or credit line purchases, and we are instructed

specifically to pay taxes: "Let no debt remain outstanding …" Rom 13:8 (NIV) When we borrow, we become slaves to the lender, which can lead to a multitude of problems in life.
4. Share joyfully. God loves a cheerful giver, someone who gives out of joy and abundance instead of obligation. Give of your money to God and to the poor. Giving is always rewarded with a blessing, even though that blessing often isn't seen or experienced immediately. Some people who have given generously throughout their lives still lose their jobs or businesses. Believers should not give out of an expectation of return, but because they understand all resources are a gift from God and are abundant in the ways they need them. Also, believers give to everyone, not only those whom they love or with whom they agree. Anyone can give generously to a certain few, but it takes true dedication to God to give to everyone equally.

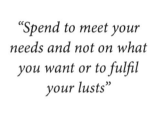

"Spend to meet your needs and not on what you want or to fulfil your lusts"

5. Spend to meet your needs and not on what you want or to fulfil your lusts.

Budgeting is an important part of marriage and an important part of planning for your marriage. You may choose to handle this in many ways, but if you need a starting point, don't fret. You can use the sample on the following template to begin your conversations about finances.

SAMPLE BUDGET CHART

MONTH OF:

GROSS INCOME (BEFORE TAXES) $_____.___

	Items	A Amt. Allocated	B Amt. Spent	C Difference
1	Tithe (10 per cent)			
2	FIXED EXPENSES			
	Taxes			
	CPP & EI			
	Other			
	Total			
	Total tithe & fixed expenses **			
	Working Income-Deduct Total			
	Tithe & Fixed Exp. from Gross			
	Gross Income			
3	**SAVINGS (10 PER CENT OF WORKING INCOME)**			
4	LIVING EXP (70 per cent of Working Income)			
	Mortgage or Rent, Prop Taxes			
	Gas/ Hydro			
	Telephone			
	Cable			
	Insurance (home, furniture)			
	Gasoline			
	Car Repairs			
	Insurance (Auto)			
	Medical			
	Food/Household			

	Clothing/Hair/Nail/Cosmetics			
	Gifts			
	Vacation			
	Allowance			
	Other			
	TOTAL LIVING EXPENSES			
5	**DEBTS (20 PER CENT OF WORKING INCOME)**			
	Visa			
	Car Loan			
	Line of Credit			
	TOTAL			
6	**SUMMARY OF ALLOCATIONS**			
	Gross Income from above			
	Total Allocated in 6 boxes in A			
	Difference (Balance or Short)			
7	**SUMMARY OF AMOUNT SPENT**			
	Gross Amount from above			
	Total Allocated in 5 boxes in B			
	Difference (Balance or Short)			

Summary

Disagreement over money can cause tension between spouses and conflict in the family. It is God's will that man be master of his domain, including his finances.

1. Remember that while love of money leads to evil, money is a necessary part of life and is provided by God.
2. Irresponsible spending can be a symptom of deeper marital, spiritual or psychological problems; dealing

with the underlying issue will help you manage your money better.
3. Budget carefully, spend realistically and share joyfully.

12

Leaving a Godly Legacy

Romans 9:29 (MSG) says: "Isaiah had looked ahead and spoken the truth: If our powerful God had not provided us a legacy of living children, we would have ended up like ghost towns, like Sodom and Gomorrah." In this verse, Paul cites Isaiah, saying that if God did not provide a lineage of people with a legacy of faith and godliness, then they would have ended up like Sodom and Gomorrah. I believe we who embrace righteousness should live with the purpose of leaving an honourable lineage for the generation after us to continue. Leaving a godly legacy starts with a passion to pursue the ways of God. It is followed by faith, vision, character, commitment and an understanding of God's purpose for our lives, including marriage (if marriage is part of God's plan for you). In Malachi 2:16 (MSG), God says: "I hate divorce…I hate the violent dismembering of the 'one flesh' of marriage. So watch yourselves. Don't let your guard down. Don't cheat."

In the dialogue with the Pharisees in Mark 10:5-9 (KJV), when they were testing Jesus and submitted that Moses authorized them to give a bill of divorce, Jesus said: "…For the hardness of your heart he wrote you this precept. But from the beginning of creation God made them male and female. For this cause shall a man leave his father and mother, and cleave to his wife; and they twain shall be one flesh: so then they are no more twain, but one flesh. What therefore God hath joined together, let not man put asunder." Remember that in Chapter 7, I mentioned leaving and cleaving applies to both parties.

In most cases divorce leaves the divorced parties, and any children of the divorced, vulnerable to much complication and greater challenges in life. Yet if they seek, find and follow God's ways they can leave an equally or more valuable legacy as they follow after the heart of God for their lives. Because of the challenges, frustrations and even the loneliness people face as a single parent or in a blended family, they may be more motivated to seek their Heavenly Father for guidance in their daily lives and consequently live out a godly legacy.

Though it is good to leave a financial inheritance for your family, a godly legacy is far more valuable. In fact, it so far surpasses the financial that the two are incomparable. Money can corrupt and is easily wasted through unwise management. A godly legacy, on the other hand, passes from generation to generation and adds not only money, but also that which money cannot buy. Proverbs 15:6 (DARBY) declares: "In the house of a righteous [man] is much treasure; but in the revenue of a wicked [man] is disturbance." A legacy is of intangible value. It could be good or bad, and it is handed down from ancestors or predecessors. As Christians, the gift we strive to leave for the generations that follow us should be a legacy of godliness. If you're wondering what a godly legacy looks like in reality, consider the examples of the Duke and Edwards families as reported on the website www.themoralliberal.com:

Max Duke was an atheist and his wife was also a godless woman. When 560 of their descendants were traced, the results were as follows:
- 7 murderers
- 60 thieves
- 50 women of debauchery
- 130 convicts
- 310 paupers
- 400 physically wrecked by overindulging

Overall, Max Duke's descendants cost the U.S. government more than $1,250,000 in the nineteenth century alone.

Jonathan Edwards, on the other hand, was a Christian and so was his wife. They strove to live a godly life and tried to raise their family to be godly people as well. When 1,394 of their descendants were traced, the results were very different:
- 294 college graduates
- 1 U.S. vice president
- 3 U.S. senators
- 3 governors
- 3 mayors
- 13 college presidents
- 30 judges
- 65 professors
- 80 policemen
- 100 lawyers

Building the kind of legacy Jonathan Edwards left for his descendants doesn't happen without hard work. It requires increasing levels of commitment from a married couple. This includes commitment by both the man and woman to spiritual maturity, their intimate personal relationship with God and each other, and sharing of unconditional love. This practice will contribute to a treasured legacy that will be a blessing to the generations that follow.

1. Commitment to spiritual maturity. John 15:4 (NIV) states: "Remain in me, as I also remain in you. No branch can bear fruit by itself; it must remain in the vine. Neither can you bear fruit unless you remain in me. Some of the most important fruit a married couple will or will not bear is in the lives of their children. In this passage from the book of John, we learn that, in order to bear any fruit, we must remain in Christ, which means we must have a working relationship with God. By following the guidance He left for us in His written, inspired word, we can be sure to nourish our intimate relationships with God and continue to bear fruit.

2. Commitment to love one another. John 15:11-12 (NIV) reads: "I have told you this so that my joy may be in you and that your joy may be complete. My command is this: Love each other as I have loved you." God loves us unconditionally and completely. God loves us enough to make the ultimate sacrifice. To love each other (spouses and children) as God loved us is a truly monumental act that will conquer all things. If we love sacrificially, without pride, hypocrisy or expectation, we give our children the best possible foundation in life. This foundation will carry them through their own lives and become the legacy you want to leave for them.

"Building a legacy of godliness also requires that you surrender to the will of God"

Building a legacy of godliness also requires that you surrender to the will of God. In Romans 12:1-2 (NIV) Paul writes: "Therefore, I urge you, brothers, in view of God's mercy, to offer your bodies as a living sacrifice, holy and pleasing to God—this is your true and proper worship. Do not conform any longer to the pattern of this world, but be transformed by the renewing of your mind. Then you will be able to test and approve what God's will is—his good, pleasing, and perfect will." God is informing us through the Apostle Paul that we cannot truly know His will until we have given up our own self-centred, egotistical plans and desires. Following the act of surrender, we will see more clearly and have a better understanding of how God wants us to live and how He will help us to do so. When we live out His will, we make progress every day toward the godly legacy we want to leave for our descendants. Even if you surrender your will and dedicate yourself to the required commitments, the journey toward a lasting legacy of godliness will be challenging. Forces of darkness are real, and they will challenge you in your goal. Paul's letter to the church at Ephesus details what you are up against:

> For our struggle is not against flesh and blood, but against the rulers, against the authorities, against the spiritual forces of evil in the heavenly realms.
>
> Therefore put on the full armour of God, so that when the day of evil comes, you may be able to stand your ground, and after you have done everything, to stand.
>
> Stand firm then, with the belt of truth buckled around your waist, with the breastplate of righteousness in place, and with your feet fitted with the readiness that comes from the gospel of peace. Ephesians 6:12-15 (NIV)

It is essential, with this knowledge, to take two actions in the rough times of your marriage:
1. Point your finger to the true enemy and accuser. Understand who your enemy is and when he is attacking you. Know not to blame your spouse for these attacks, but instead the invisible evil forces.
2. Don't wait for your spouse to act or even to acknowledge the attacks you are under. Do what God demands of you and your spouse will catch up to you. It is important to know your spouse sometimes may not have the clarity to know you are under attack. At other times, you may be the one who struggles. However, in either situation, if the person who does understand acts quickly and righteously, the Devil's forces can be successfully battled.

CONTRAST BETWEEN A WORLDLY LEGACY AND A GODLY LEGACY

(as cited in Family Life Marriage Conference workbook)

	WORLDLY LEGACY	GODLY LEGACY
Perspective on marriage: **MOTIVATION** **METHOD**	 • To gratify self • Promote the self	 • To glorify God • Promote oneness with spouse
Purpose of marriage:	• Have own needs met • Achieve romantic dream • Sex multiplicity	• Mirror God's image • Mutually complete one another • Godly legacy
Plan:	• 50/50 performance	• 100/100 performance

CONTRAST BETWEEN A WORLDLY LEGACY AND A GODLY LEGACY
(as cited in Family Life Marriage Conference workbook)

	WORLDLY LEGACY	**GODLY LEGACY**
Plan:	• "Will never happen to me"	• Acceptance
	• Based on feelings	• Established commitments
	• Conditional commitment	• Unconditional commitment
Power:	• Flesh	• God's spirit
Results:	• Tribute to family	• Tribute to God
	• Turmoil and division	• Peace and harmony

In order to accomplish the goal of building this lasting, godly legacy, couples must reaffirm their commitment to each other as often as necessary. Do this in private and in public. Let your spouse know every day that you are still committed to him/her and the marriage. Always keep God's purpose and plan foremost in your view. Practise healthy communication, develop your oneness, be careful to practise stewardship with your finances, and aim to leave a godly legacy. It will affect the generations to follow, and a portrait of your life will be hung on the wall of eternity. Something to remember at this point: when you were born, after your first breath, you cried yet those around you rejoiced; but at the end of your life on earth as you exit to the other side, most of your loved ones around you will cry yet if you leave a good legacy you and God will rejoice.

Summary

1. A godly legacy is a far more important inheritance to leave for your children than a financial one.
2. Building a godly legacy isn't easy and requires both partners to be fully committed to their own spiritual development and that of their children.
   - Commit to being spiritually mature.
   - Commit to loving one another unconditionally.
   - Surrender to the will of God.

The journey toward a lasting godly legacy is challenging even when you commit yourself completely; the forces of darkness will challenge you. Strive to recognize when you are under attack from evil, and don't blame your spouse for the work of dark forces.

Conclusion

It is understandable if you're feeling a bit apprehensive at this stage. After all, for the last twelve chapters we have been discussing the challenges and issues that you will face as you enter your marriage—issues that may seem intimidating if you haven't considered them before. Remember, though, that these challenges have always and will always be there. Ignoring the potential issues will not help your marriage to succeed. Knowing about and anticipating the challenges you will face will help you prepare for your future and ultimately triumph over the dark forces working against godly marriage.

In the introduction, I talked about marriage as a blood covenant with God at its centre. God's purpose for marriage, as described in Chapter 1, is for life-long unity between a man and a woman. Men and women need each other to be truly complete in order to achieve their full potential and to be fruitful and multiply as God commanded. Although it is a challenge to enter into and maintain a godly marriage, it stretches us to live out our God-given potential. It is important to keep in mind the benefits, both spiritual and practical, that a healthy and godly marriage bring you and your descendants. Remember what was said in 1 Corinthians 11:11 (NIV): "… in the Lord woman is not independent of man, nor is man independent of woman." Eve was made to be a suitable companion to Adam because he needed companionship. To truly live in God's image, man and woman must join together as one. Only then will you be able to realize your full potential.

Communication and honesty are the ultimate keys to a successful, happy and long-lasting marriage. As I talked about in Chapter 4, this starts even before you say "I do." Seeking pre-marriage counselling from your pastor or a professional can help you establish this open communication before you get to the altar. Regardless of whether you look for assistance from outside the marriage, however, speaking candidly with each other about your plans for the future is vital to avoiding issues later on in your relationship. Remember the saying "love is blind" can be a double-edged sword. On the one hand, it means you and your spouse can look past each other's shortcomings and appreciate each other for your true potential. On the other, it means that infatuation can make you blind to compatibility issues that could become big problems later down the line. Getting an outside perspective can help you to identify these potential problems, both before the marriage starts and as it progresses.

Remember there is no such thing as a conflict-free marriage. Even when there is great love between two compatible people, conflicts will arise in the course of making your life together. Addressing conflicts as they arise in a productive rather than a hurtful way is one of the most important skills to develop. The communication techniques outlined in Chapters 4, 5 and 6 of this book can serve as excellent guidelines for effective lifelong communication.

Godly marriage is a life-long journey with vast spiritual rewards. Marriage gives you a partner for all of your endeavours, contributing to both your worldly success and the growth of your own relationship with the Heavenly Father. By joining together, you and your partner will be better able to face and conquer the dark forces at work in the world. The family unit of a man, a woman and their children is a God-given recipe for life-long happiness, a definition that has endured across the centuries despite the modern secular attempts to alter the meaning and purpose of marriage. By holding firm to marriage as a covenant between not only man and wife, but also man, wife and God, the benefits of marriage will extend beyond this life. Consider again the comparison made in Chapter 12 between the godless legacy of Max Duke and the godly legacy of Jonathan Edwards. The work required to embark upon a godly marriage has rewards that will extend beyond your own life to those of your children and your children's children and bring an enduring legacy of Christian love and goodwill, rooted in honesty and obedience to the Lord's will.

"Nothing great has ever come without great challenges… but with God's on your side, all things are possible"

Nothing great has ever come without great challenges. Wherever you are in the journey of godly marriage—whether you're looking for a partner, planning your wedding day, approaching your ten-year anniversary or considering a second union—it is my sincere hope that the advice given in this book will help you find the lasting joy that all men and women were designed by God to find in the covenant of marriage. Successful marriage isn't easy, but with God's on your side, all things are possible.

CPSIA information can be obtained
at www.ICGtesting.com
Printed in the USA
LVHW01s1722230817
546007LV00021BA/208/P